Successful Job Hunting
In A Week

Hilton Catt and Patricia Scudamore

The Teach Yourself series has been trusted around the world
for over 60 years. This new series of 'In A Week' business books
is designed to help people at all levels and around the world to
further their careers. Learn in a week what the experts learn in
a lifetime.

Hilton Catt and Patricia Scudamore have operated in the employment field for many years. They run their own business, the Scudamore Catt Partnership. They have written a number of books on career management, including other titles in the *In A Week* series.

Successful
Job Hunting

Hilton Catt
and
Patricia Scudamore

www.inaweek.co.uk

Hodder Education

338 Euston Road, London NW1 3BH

Hodder Education is an Hachette UK company

First published in UK 2000 by Hodder Education

Previous editions of this book were published by Hodder in 2000 and 2002

This edition published 2012

Hachette UK's policy is to use papers that are natural, renewable and recyclable products and made from wood grown in sustainable forests. The logging and manufacturing processes are expected to conform to the environmental regulations of the country of origin.

www.hoddereducation.co.uk

Typeset by Cenveo Publisher Services

Printed and bound by CPI Group (UK) Ltd, Croydon, CR0 4YY.

Contents

Introduction

In *Successful Job Hunting In A Week* you will learn everything
you need to know about successful job hunting. Starting on
Sunday, read the book a chapter a day and see how quickly
you build up an expert inside knowledge of how the job
market works. Then as the week goes by, discover how you
can apply the knowledge you have acquired and use it to your
advantage. By the end of Saturday you will find that you have
a formidable store of practical information at your fingertips
for dealing with the tough challenges that all serious job
hunters have to face sooner or later.

Whether you are a newcomer to the world of work or a second,
third or fourth jobber, you will find plenty here for you. Whether
you are simply looking to better yourself, are facing redundancy
or trying to break into an entirely new field – in fact, whatever your
situation is – the task of finding opportunities that are consistent
with the aim you have set yourself is still the same.

On **Sunday** and **Monday**, we will introduce you to the nature
of the job market and some fundamental rules for anyone
engaged in the task of job hunting.

Then, on **Tuesday**, you will find a whole chapter devoted to
getting you to see the benefits of giving your job hunting a
sense of direction – a process we call targeting. You will learn
on Tuesday how to target jobs properly and, from carrying out a
simple exercise, you will immediately see the benefits such as:

- less time wasting and better results for your effort
- fewer 'sorry but no thank you letters' of the type that, over
  time, can lead to discouragement and giving up
- a truer picture of what the market for someone like you has
  to offer
- more accurate feedback – feedback you can use to give your
  targeting the fine-tuning it needs
- most importantly, more success: more job applications with
  positive outcomes.

On **Wednesday** you will teach yourself what it takes and how to overcome competition of the type you will face in abundance when you apply for any good job that has been advertised.

But is it true that the best jobs are never advertised? The short answer is 'yes' and by the end of **Thursday** you will know all about this so-called invisible job market – why it exists and, most importantly, what you have to do to access it. You will learn about proactive sourcing, which is a collective term to describe the methods that you can use to tap into the invisible market – a market that would remain hidden from you if you did not take active steps to engage with it.

On **Friday** you will discover how to put an added dimension into your search for the job of your dreams by boosting your chances of being headhunted.

Finally, on **Saturday** you will teach yourself what to do when the job offer is put in your hands and you have to make your mind up whether to say 'yes' or 'no'. It may seem like a straightforward decision but always at the back of your mind is the fear of a step into the unknown and the risk of making a bad move. You'll find how to assess the risk of changing jobs properly and, where there are danger signs, how to recognize them.

Hilton Catt and Patricia Scudamore

SUNDAY

Understanding today's job market

Today you will learn about how the job market is made up of two sectors:

1 **The visible market**: the jobs that are advertised in newspapers, or on the Internet or anywhere else where they are open for everyone to see. Here the challenge is engaging and seeing off competition, especially where the jobs are good jobs.

2 **The invisible market**: the jobs that are rumoured to be the best jobs; the jobs that, for one reason or another, employers keep to themselves. Here the challenge is finding out about these jobs and, when you have, knowing what to do to get your face in the frame.

Just as the visible and invisible markets are very different, so are the techniques you have to use to engage with them:

Reactive sourcing is how you access jobs on the visible market.

Proactive sourcing is how you access jobs on the invisible market.

The terms 'reactive sourcing' and 'proactive sourcing' will come up again and again, both in today's lesson and as you move through the rest of the week. It is important today that you get used to the terms and understand what they mean and to what they refer.

The job jungle

Imagine you're setting off on a journey through the jungle all on your own. The first few steps you take will be bold ones until you find out the jungle is a strange place where there are no paths to follow and no signposts to show you the way. You press on regardless, hoping everything will be OK, but after a while you're thrashing around in the undergrowth hopelessly lost. Sooner or later despair takes over and all you want is the quickest way out.

Going out on to today's job market can be a bit like this. At times it seems impenetrable and hostile. At times it feels like all you're doing is going round in circles and achieving nothing. At times all you will want to do is sit down on the ground and put your head in your hands.

WARNING!
Discouragement *is what happens to people who thrash around in the job jungle with no clear sense of direction. In job hunting, discouragement is what you need to avoid at all costs.*

Job hunter's concerns

A few years ago we asked a random sample of candidates for junior to middle management posts in a manufacturing industry to list what concerned them most about today's job market conditions. This is what they came up with:

- the sheer volume of competition for good jobs – the difficulty in even getting interviews
- bad manners (employers not replying to applications or letting candidates know how they got on at interviews)
- the so-called invisible market – the rumoured 90 per cent of jobs that aren't advertised; how to find out about such jobs
- the risk attached to changing jobs; the fear of making bad moves and what could follow.

Understanding today's job market

So what's going on here and why do so many people see today's job market as such a 'difficult' place? Let's take a closer look and see what we can find out.

Few of us need any reminding that the world in which we live and work has changed very substantially in the last 20 years. Big smokestack industries have for the large part gone. Dozens and dozens of small start-up businesses have taken their place – to the extent that the small firm sector is now an important provider of quality employment (a fact no one should ignore).

Even with big firms, the need to cut costs has driven many of them to downsize and streamline. What's more, this downsizing and streamlining has been accompanied in many cases by breaking up once large structures into smaller, more manageable units (fragmentation).

How do these changes affect the way recruitment is handled?

Classic recruitment

We have coined this term to describe most people's conception of what the recruitment process involves. The following example will help you understand what it is.

Recruitment today

Big companies Classic recruitment still goes on, of course, but in many big companies where classic recruitment used to be practised, very different circumstances now prevail.

For a start, human resources departments suffered more than most in the various phases of headcount slashing we have seen in recent years. Viewed as peripheral to the core activity of businesses, they have, in some cases, been disposed of altogether while in others they have been reduced to mere shadows of their former selves. The result? We see recruitment today pushed more and more on to the shoulders of line managers, meaning the standard to which it is done depends on:

 ● how much time and what resources they can give it (bearing in mind they have other functions to discharge as well), *and*
 ● how experienced they are.

Time and resources are, of course, major areas of concern for all practising managers but, to add to the problems, the delayerings, restructurings and downsizings of recent years have left many of them with little or nothing in the way of administrative support. Witness the fact that the armies of secretaries and assistants who once used to surround senior managers in big companies have to all intents and purposes gone. Today the same senior managers are more likely to have to do their own fetching and carrying, take their own phone calls and, in some cases, type their own letters as well.

Small companies Small companies have never carried human resources departments (at least not as a rule). Recruitment has always been dealt with by busy managers with other responsibilities. What's different about small companies is that there are a lot more of them about.

Bad manners?

Why are employers so remiss about responding to applications these days? Has there been an outbreak of bad manners as some job hunters seem to think?

Not that we wish to excuse employers who don't reply to candidates' letters but the explanation, very often, is not rudeness but some hard-pressed manager faced with the problem of finding a replacement for a key member of staff who has decided to leave. What happens is this. An ad is put in the paper and maybe a few firms of recruitment consultants are contacted. Where the job is a good job, the result is a glut of applications. Bearing in mind that our manager is probably not too used to such situations, they respond by picking out a couple of letters which catch their eye then put the rest to one side with the intention of dealing with them later. Another crisis crops up followed by another and, like any good manager, they respond by prioritizing. As a result, jobs like replying to a bunch of unsuccessful applicants get pushed to the bottom of the pile from where they may never surface.

Quick fixes

Another facet of the downsized delayered world we live in is the way gaps in the ranks of key people quickly cause companies problems.

Example: Company Y

Company Y is a manufacturing plant employing 600 people. Previously Company Y had a three-tier management structure:

Manufacturing Director

▼

Section managers (5)

▼

Cell managers (30)

Five years ago, faced with intense global competition and the urgent need to cut operating costs, Company Y decided to take out the section management tier from its structure, leaving cell managers reporting directly to the Manufacturing Director. As a consequence of this, wherever a cell manager's position is vacant, shop floor personnel have a direct line to the Manufacturing Director – a situation the Manufacturing Director finds difficult to deal with. A further consequence? The Manufacturing Director does his level best to get any vacant cell manager slot filled as quickly as he can.

The invisible job market

Classic recruitment is time-consuming and hard work. It has little appeal therefore to hard-pressed managers with vacancies that need filling fast and a thousand and one other concerns clamouring for their attention. So what happens in these situations? The answer is they do what all resourceful managers do. They look for short cuts.

Here is an example of a short cut:

'If we advertise positions in the press we find ourselves inundated with response – 90 per cent of which is totally unsuitable. Rather than give ourselves this kind of hassle we prefer first of all to see if there is anyone we know in the trade. If there isn't, we usually go to a few firms of recruitment consultants and ask them to put up a shortlist of candidates from their files.'

A vast and largely untapped invisible job market has emerged in recent years – jobs that are never advertised and are filled by one of three methods:

1 **Approach** – companies sourcing people through their networks of contacts within given industries or trades or using headhunters to do this task for them.
2 **Recruitment consultants** – accessing candidates by asking firms of recruitment consultants to search their files for suitable candidates.
3 **Previous applicants** – revisiting previous applicants including unsolicited CVs.

There are other reasons apart from the ones we have touched on already for the growth in the invisible market.

Let three senior executives from the new breed of small knowledge-based businesses explain:

'The people we're interested in won't necessarily be looking for another job. This is why advertising doesn't work for us.'

'We're seeking people with scarce and very defined skills. We find the only way of getting such people is by going to specialist firms of recruitment consultants.'

'Picking up a square peg in a senior management job is a major area of concern for us because of the damage it could do to a team-based business like this. When we recruit, therefore, we always enlist the help of headhunters. We feel happier about people who come to us with a headhunter's recommendation.'

The key points to pick out here are:

- the increased awareness today of the downsides of making poor selection decisions, particularly where the vacant slot is a position of responsibility; not only is there the damage to the business to be considered but also the prospect of litigation if the bad choice has to be exited quickly
- the impact of skills shortages on businesses: the widely held view that recruiting people with scarce skills calls for something 'special'
- the growth of headhunting as a preferred method of recruiting, particularly where senior executive appointments are concerned; the 'comfort' factor that headhunting offers.

There are just three things you need to appreciate about the invisible market:

1 it's big
2 it's getting bigger
3 you need to get in on it.

Reactive and proactive sourcing

The last job for today is to introduce you to some useful terminology.

Reactive sourcing

This is where the stimulus is provided by the employer – usually in the form of advertising. Here you are responding to an invitation to put yourself forward and the quality of your response is what counts. Reactive sourcing is used to attack the visible market.

Proactive sourcing

This is job hunting aimed at the invisible market – where, to penetrate the walls and get your face in the frame, the stimulus needs to come from you.

Successful job hunting today means having the capacity to attack both the visible and the invisible markets, which in turn means using a 'mix 'n' match' of proactive and reactive sourcing. Too many candidates put all their effort into the latter (replying to advertisements), meaning they miss out on some of the better opportunities the market offers.

Summary

One of the reasons why candidates prefer to put their effort into reactive sourcing is because, on the face of it, it is easy. All you have to do is sit at home and flick through the local evening paper on jobs night, comb through the ads in your professional journals, check out a few websites and there you have it. Job done, or so you think, whereas in reality all you have looked at is a tiny fragment of what's out there for you. By completely ignoring the invisible market you have effectively put a barrier between yourself and what could be the best of what the market in its complete state has to offer.

The conclusion to what we have done today is therefore that the job market is like any other market. You don't dictate the way it works. It has its own rules and you have to learn to play by them or you will find yourself constantly in situations where, unless luck is on your side, you will end up banging your head on brick walls.

The message? Adapt your job hunting strategies to how the market works today and not to the way it was years ago. Learn to move with the times. Don't get left behind.

SUNDAY
MONDAY
TUESDAY
WEDNESDAY
THURSDAY
FRIDAY
SATURDAY

Fact-check (answers at the back)

1. The best jobs are found on the Internet. Do you...
   a) Agree? ❏
   b) Agree strongly? ❏
   c) Disagree? ❏
   d) Have no opinion? ❏

2. What percentage of jobs are never advertised?
   a) Over 90% ❏
   b) 75–90% ❏
   c) 50–75% ❏
   d) Under 50% ❏

3. You wrote off for a job that you saw advertised. Four weeks passed and you heard nothing. When you ring the firm's human resources department you are told the job has been filled. Do you...
   a) Ask why your application has been unsuccessful? ❏
   b) Ask why they didn't let you know? ❏
   c) Ask both a) and b)? ❏
   d) Say thank you and goodbye? ❏

4. Where do you find invisible market jobs advertised?
   a) On the Internet ❏
   b) You don't find them Advertised ❏
   c) In newspapers ❏
   d) Don't know ❏

5. Which of the following is an example of reactive sourcing?
   a) Registering with an agency ❏
   b) Calling companies to see if they have any vacancies ❏
   c) Looking at employers' websites ❏
   d) Sending in an unsolicited CV ❏

6. Which of the following is an example of proactive sourcing?
   a) Replying to advertisements in professional journals ❏
   b) Doing nothing ❏
   c) Asking round your colleagues and contacts ❏
   d) None of the above ❏

7. What is 'approach'?
   a) Replying to an advertisement and being asked to attend an interview ❏
   b) A friend asking you to help them find a job ❏
   c) What recruitment consultants do ❏
   d) Employers using their contacts to source staff ❏

8. In what order should you do your sourcing?
   a) Reactive sourcing first ❏
   b) Proactive sourcing first ❏
   c) Both at the same time ❏
   d) It depends ❏

9. You apply for 50 jobs and don't get a single interview. Do you...
   a) Keep going? ❏
   b) Take stock first then keep going? ❏
   c) Give up? ❏
   d) Go down the pub? ❏

10. You send in an unsolicited CV and hear nothing. Do you...
    a) Ring in and ask if it has been received ❏
    b) As a) but complain ❏
    c) Send in another unsolicited CV ❏
    d) Do nothing ❏

SUN
MONDAY
TUESDAY
WEDNESDAY
THURSDAY
FRIDAY
SATURDAY

MONDAY

Availability, accessibility and application

Today you will learn three important rules for going out on the job market. They are:

Availability The importance of 'being there' and being contactable when employers want to speak to you. The importance of being available to go to interviews at times when employers choose.

Accessibility The importance of making yourself understood to employers so it is clear to them who you are, where you are coming from and what you are seeking to achieve.

Application The importance of putting all your effort into job hunting and not treating it as something that you pick up when you feel like it and put it down again when you are less inclined.

These rules – known collectively as the **'Three As'** – are central to successful job hunting in the market conditions that prevail today and in this chapter we will spend time looking at each of them more closely.

By the end of today you will be able to see for yourself where, without knowing it, you might be putting obstacles in the way of employers who are trying to engage with you. If you are, then before you go any further you need to take steps to clear the obstacles out of the way.

Availability

Being in the right place at the right time helps with most things in life and job hunting is no exception. Being there, being easy for employers to contact, having the capacity to attend interviews as and when required, all go a long way to ensuring successful outcomes in today's market conditions. This is why you need to audit your availability before you set foot into the job market, i.e. before lack of availability becomes the reason for you not having much joy.

How do you do this? Go through the following checklist and answer the questions as truthfully as you can.

Availability checklist

● How would prospective employers get on if they needed to get hold of you in a hurry? Would they have your email or phone numbers where they could contact you?

● Similarly, if the same employers needed to speak to you out of hours, would they have phone numbers or your home email where you could be reached?

● Could contacting you involve hassle in the shape of phones that aren't answered or lines that are engaged for long periods?

● What would your answer be if an employer needed to get you in for an interview in office hours some time within the next seven days? Would you be able to get the time off work or would it be difficult for you?

Going through this checklist will help you to expose flaws in your availability. Hopefully, it will also throw up some points for action such as:

● redoing your CV so that all telephone points of contact are included – by this we mean your home, work and mobile telephone numbers. In the case of your home number, you also need to give an indication of the time when you normally get in (e.g. 'after 6.30 p.m.').
● making sure all your phone numbers have voicemail
● making sure you check your email and voicemail messages regularly
● making sure you check for any missed calls

- introducing a few disciplines at home such as telling members of the family to keep their phone conversations brief, especially early in the evening (when people like employers, headhunters and recruitment consultants could be trying to get through)
- always keeping back a few days' holiday in case you need to go for interviews
- cleaning up your answer tape – with the prospect of employers, recruitment consultants and headhunters ringing you up, now's the time to take those silly messages off your voicemail!

Make yourself available

Lack of availability sometimes has unusual causes. Often you are the last to find out about them.

Today the phone is used more and more for contacting job applicants. This is, in part, a reflection of the instantaneous, paper-free world we live in, in part the pressure on management time, and in part the increasing involvement of people like headhunters who do most of their business on the phone. As a consequence, interview lists are frequently decided on the basis of who can be contacted and who can't. Candidates who are difficult to get hold of are candidates who get given the miss.

Accessibility

A prospective employer needs to be able to see who you are, where you are coming from and what you are capable of doing in a very compressed period of time. Needless to say, accessibility has got a lot to do with the design of your CV. It has particular relevance to two situations:

1 **Visible market:** where you are applying for a good job which has been widely advertised. Here the problem is going to be competition. You will be one of many applicants and somehow your CV has got to stand out from the rest.
2 **Invisible market:** where you're mailshotting your CV to employers on the off chance that there may be something suitable for you. Unsolicited CVs tend to get the 'quick read' treatment, so, again, they need to catch the reader's eye to prevent them from being binned instantly.

Revisiting your CV

It goes almost without saying that you won't get very far on your trip into the job jungle without a CV. If you don't have an up-to-date CV, for any reason, then take steps to get one prepared. Most people already have a CV. The task for them, therefore, is to take a critical look at what they've got and to see how it stands up from an accessibility point of view. Here to help you do this is a list of common accessibility problems. As far as your CV is concerned, see if any of the caps fit and, if they do, take the necessary action.

Again, do this before you attempt to set foot in the job market.

- **Too long** Anything over three sheets of A4 is suspect. Long CVs don't get read or don't get read properly. Equally, don't go to the other extreme and put your whole life on to half a page of A4. From an accessibility point of view, CVs that are too short are no better than ones that are too long.
- **Too inconcise** Long, rambling descriptions tend to lose the reader's attention. For example, the detail of what you did in a job ten years ago isn't likely to be of much interest to anyone.

- **Too much jargon** Some recipients of your CV will be generalists – e.g. human resources managers and selection consultants. Bear this in mind and use terminology that people from all backgrounds can understand.
- **No clear statement of your aims** Someone who reads your CV needs to know what you're hoping to achieve by changing jobs. If you're looking for more money, for example, you need to make this clear by stating the figure you have in mind. (This point will come up again tomorrow when we look at targeting jobs.)
- **Poor presentation** This is usually the result of trying to cram in too much information into too little space. Narrow margins, small font sizes of the sort that have readers searching frantically for their glasses (or conversely not bothering), lack of white space on the page – these are all factors which detract from your CV being a quick and easy read. The answer? Edit furiously. Stick to presenting an overview and leave out the reams of detail.
- **Lack of logical order** CVs that 'jump about' fail on accessibility – for example, CVs that intersperse education and qualifications with information about experience gained during employment. Don't confuse your readers. Surprisingly, lack of logical order is the commonest problem with CVs.
- **Not customized** Don't use the same CV for every job application you make. Let the wonders of modern software help you customize your CV to the job you're applying for (more on this subject later in the week).

TIP

Be bold

Don't fight shy of making radical changes to the layout of your CV. Even if you've paid a small fortune to have your CV professionally prepared, don't hesitate to chop it about if you feel aims, achievements and qualifications don't come across sufficiently clearly.

A useful image to have in mind as you go through your CV is that of some stressed-out overworked senior executive given the task of wading through a hundred job applications with a view to picking out a few for interview. Just to add a bit of flavour, let's say our senior executive decides to leave this task till the end of the day when the telephone traffic has died down but when he won't be at his best for giving his full and undivided attention. Typically, he'll cast his eye over each application searching out key points that look OK (e.g. a certain type of experience). From this quick flick through he'll put the applications into three piles: the ones that interest him, the don't-knows, and the no-hopers. When he's finished doing this, he'll probably look at the 'yes' pile again just to make doubly sure he's picked out the right people. If the 'yes' pile thus reduced happens to coincide with what our senior executive views as a reasonable number of people to call in for interview, that will be that as far as the preliminary sifting process is concerned – i.e. the don't-knows will be joining the unsuitables in the turndown pile. If the pile is a bit thin on numbers, however, the don't-knows might just get a second airing.

The point to grasp? That even though all recruitment may not be dealt with in this way, your CV has still got to be capable of surviving this kind of treatment. It has got to hit our weary senior executive in the eye first time because, if it doesn't, it stands a good chance of ending up in places where it is unlikely to ever see the light of day again.

Before leaving our senior executive to his after-hours reading, it is worth pondering on the fact that, once he's finished putting his interview list together, he could round off the evening by ringing the candidates he's picked out. Here is where your availability comes in. The ones he manages to contact will be invited for interview. The ones he doesn't may not get another chance.

Application

One of the big challenges you face on your journey through the job jungle is having the tenacity to keep going and not be put off by any of the difficulties that you encounter. Partly this is to do with avoiding discouragement and partly to do with keeping your expectations in line. With the latter:

- don't expect to be invited for an interview every time you apply for a job (it won't happen)
- don't expect everyone to be nice to you.

Picking up on the second of these points, employers' standards vary enormously and not all the treatment you receive will be to your liking. The mistake, however, is to let bad experiences get to you so they become a source of discouragement and a reason for you throwing in the towel prematurely.

Employers who don't reply

Going back to yesterday, we saw the concerns about employers who don't reply to applications or don't let candidates know how they got on at interviews. We saw at the same time, however, that these omissions are not always manifestations of bad manners – as some job hunters seem to think – but evidence of organizations in turmoil or managers under pressure – in short, nothing very unusual in the modern-day business world.

The message? Don't get wound up about employers whose communication skills are lacking, and to some extent condition yourself to accepting this kind of treatment as the norm. Certainly don't let the general standards of employers' behaviour become the reason for you giving up because you feel you can't take any more.

Prepare for the hard knocks

Even if you can learn to live with employers who don't reply to your applications, because of its diversity the modern job market can still be a hostile and unpredictable place. Expect, therefore, your path to success to be littered with bad interview experiences and brushes with employers who don't seem to know what they're doing. Try to find ways of hardening yourself against the knocks.

Anything else?

What other preparations do you need to make before you set out on your job hunting expedition?

Time off work

Having the capacity to take time off work to attend interviews is, as we have seen, an important part of your availability and, for this reason, you must always keep back a few days of your holiday entitlement.

The point stretches a little further, however. As part of your preparations for going out on to the job market, you must condition yourself into viewing your time off work as precious and something not to be squandered. An example of squandering time off work is using it to attend interviews for jobs that wouldn't interest you even if they were offered to you. We will be exploring this use of time off work in more detail tomorrow when we will be looking at targeting (making sure the jobs you're applying for are the right jobs).

For most of us, the time we can get off work is limited and even stock excuses like 'going to see the dentist' can start to wear thin after they've been used a few times. Not all employers will be happy to do interviews out of hours and this is certainly something you shouldn't be banking on.

Giving up smoking

While smoking in workplaces is banned in many countries where this book will be read, there is still concern on the part of many employers about the image of the business projected by the familiar huddle of smokers outside the front entrance to the offices. The question 'Do you smoke?' is therefore one that employers often ask at interviews or on their application forms. So much the better, for you, therefore, if you can answer truthfully 'No' and better for your health too.

Non-smokers

If you don't smoke, advertise the fact somewhere on your CV – for example, in the section giving details of your medical history. Who knows, it might just tip the balance when it comes to deciding whether to include you on the interview list or not.

Summary

Availability, accessibility and application are about accepting the realities of life in the business world we live in today. Managers with positions to fill are often working under pressure so that candidates who are seen as 'difficult' won't hold much appeal. 'Difficult' in this context includes:

● candidates who don't return their voicemail messages the same day
● candidates who want to attend interviews only at times when it suits them
● candidates who start laying down conditions (e.g. 'I will only take time off work to come for an interview if you tell me what the pay is first')
● candidates whose CVs are a jumble and need reading more than once.

Where a job is a good job and where it has been advertised (typical visible market situation), competition is always going to be an issue. Here is where you will score heavily if you can offer availability and accessibility.

The third of the three As – application – is about keeping going and not letting turn-down letters and bad interview experiences put you off. Don't expect the job market to be nice to you – not all the time.

SUNDAY
MONDAY
TUESDAY
WEDNESDAY
THURSDAY
FRIDAY
SATURDAY

Fact-check (answers at the back)

1. You miss out on an interview because the employer could not contact you. Do you...
   a) Feel it is the employer's fault? ❏
   b) Feel it is your fault? ❏
   c) At the same time as b), take steps to make sure it doesn't happen again? ❏
   d) Shrug it off? ❏

2. An employer asks you to go for an interview but you can't get time off work because you have used up all your holidays. Do you...
   a) Tell the employer you will attend only if the interview can be held on a Saturday morning? ❏
   b) Tell your boss you have a dental appointment? ❏
   c) Give the interview a miss? ❏
   d) Put your job hunting on hold until you have got some holiday back? ❏

3. What is the commonest problem with CVs?
   a) Too long ❏
   b) Lack of logical order ❏
   c) Poorly presented ❏
   d) Spelling mistakes ❏

4. You go for an interview and you are kept waiting for an hour because the applicant before you arrived late. Do you...
   a) Sit patiently? ❏
   b) Walk out? ❏
   c) Feel it is a bad reflection on the employer? ❏
   d) Complain? ❏

5. Which of the 'three As' is the most important?
   a) Availability ❏
   b) Accessibility ❏
   c) Application ❏
   d) All of them ❏

6. What is the method of contacting job applicants that employers use most?
   a) Phone ❏
   b) Email ❏
   c) Text message ❏
   d) Letter ❏

7. You want to send out a batch of unsolicited CVs. Which of the following methods will guarantee you get a reply?
   a) Emailing your CV ❏
   b) Putting it in the post with a stamped addressed envelope ❏
   c) Sending it on a fax ❏
   d) None of the above ❏

8. You don't want to receive phone calls at work. Do you...
   a) Leave your mobile number off your CV? ❏
   b) Include it but indicate that it is only to be used after 6 p.m. ❏
   c) Turn off the ring tone and pick up any missed calls and voicemail messages ❏
   d) Keep your phone switched off when you are at work ❏

9. When should you expect employers to ring you?
a) Between 9 a.m. and 6 p.m. on weekdays ❑
b) Up to 7 p.m. on weekdays ❑
c) At any time ❑
d) As b), but on Saturday mornings as well ❑

10. How many versions of your CV do you need?
a) One ❑
b) One for every application ❑
c) Five ❑
d) Ten maximum ❑

SUNDAY

MONDAY

TUESDAY

WEDNESDAY

THURSDAY

FRIDAY

SATURDAY

TUESDAY

Targeting the right jobs

Today you will learn about targeting. Targeting is what gives your job hunting its sense of direction.

Targeting is simple – so simple it is surprising that, in the true sense of what is involved, more people don't do it.

Targeting is about being clear about what you are looking for, so you know from the outset which jobs you should be applying for and which you should be leaving alone. By targeting properly your effort is therefore focused and not spread out. You get out of the habit of seeing job hunting as an exercise in chalking up how many applications you can send off. Instead, you are selective and, as you will soon see, there are enormous benefits in using this picky and choosy approach.

Targeting is an exercise that you need to carry out before you set out on your perilous expedition into the job jungle. Otherwise you run the risk of thrashing round aimlessly, and then, when you see what little progress you have made, you end up giving in. Worse still, you will see your expedition as wasted effort and it may put you off trying again.

Aims of targeting

Targeting has two aims:

- **Reducing failure** Not getting chosen for interview or going for an interview and finding you don't get put on the shortlist has a discouraging and demoralizing effect. The less of this you have to deal with, the better.
- **Reducing time-wasting** Job hunting is time-consuming. The time you give it has to be put to most effective use.

Targeting is about being *selective* with your job applications. Applying for hundreds and hundreds of jobs just because they happen to be there has no virtue to it at all. You succeed in doing nothing except:

- chalking up large numbers of 'sorry but no thank you' letters (inviting discouragement)
- frittering away your time off work time on utterly pointless interviews (loss of an important part of your availability).

Realism

Targeting needs to be done in the context of what the job market can reasonably be expected to deliver. If you set off in pursuit of unattainable targets, then, practically speaking, it is almost as bad as setting off with no targets at all.

Jobs you can't do

Although we're all entitled to have our dreams, there are some jobs that quite clearly we can't do because we don't have the necessary experience or qualifications. These jobs that are out of our range are usually self-evident to us, but occasionally we need reminding that we may be trying to take a step too far.

The signs of over-reaching? Inevitability, the number of applications where you find you don't even get as far as the interview list. The big danger in over-reaching, however, is that if you carry on doing it, you finish up feeling dejected and discouraged. The answer is, therefore, to take stock from time to time. If your job hunting has been largely fruitless, ask

SUNDAY

MONDAY

TUESDAY

WEDNESDAY

THURSDAY

FRIDAY

SATURDAY

yourself if you could be falling into the trap of applying for jobs you can't do. This is a case of acting on the feedback that the market is providing you with – feedback that's telling you you're trying to achieve something that's unattainable.

 WARNING!
In a world where selection standards are not always consistent, there is the chance you could be offered a job that's beyond your capabilities. If you accept, needless to say, your celebrations are likely to be short-lived. Your lack of capability will be found out pretty quickly and it won't be too surprising if you find yourself on the receiving end of the short, sharp exit treatment.

Jobs that don't exist

Incredible though it sounds, there are a lot of people out there pursuing jobs that don't exist or jobs that are in very short supply. Here are a few examples:

● Doug – who wants a job where he doesn't have to do shifts but where, at the same time, he won't have to take a drop in the high level of earnings he gets for working unsociable hours.
● Gaenor – who works in customer support and who wants a job where she can have every Wednesday off to go to college.

- John – who makes good money doing work he finds boring. John wants to make a complete change in career without having to take a drop in his earnings.
- Steve – who wants a senior management job where he won't have to put up with the hassle he gets now.
- Ruth – who wants a high-powered career in marketing without having to travel any further than ten miles from where she lives.

The conditions that Doug, Gaenor and the others are imposing on the jobs they're looking for effectively wipe out most, if not all, of the available market. What they are attempting to do really is dictate to the market and, not surprisingly, it doesn't work.

The lesson? Again, listen carefully to the feedback. What is it telling you? Could it be telling you, for example, that what employers have to offer and what you are looking for simply don't match up? If it does, stop what you're doing immediately and take stock. The mistake – and plenty make it – is to flog on in pursuit of these near-impossible aims year after year till discouragement sets in.

Feedback

Feedback or experience is an important part of job hunting because, at the outset, few of us have any meaningful idea of what the market for our particular talents really has to offer. What all successful job hunters do is learn from their experience and, in this way, accumulate quite formidable stores of knowledge on the demand for people in their niche occupational area. Listening to feedback is therefore important. Ignoring it is something you do at your peril.

Targeting benchmarks

Having dealt with the problems of targeting jobs you can't do and jobs that don't exist (or only exist in very small numbers), we want to turn our attention to looking at how to set about targeting jobs properly. To do this we need you to get some fixed points of reference, or benchmarks, in your mind. Targeting benchmarks will be there to help you when it comes to deciding which jobs to apply for and which to leave alone. They will help you to deal with people like recruitment consultants (people who will be using their contacts and know-how to search for jobs on your behalf). They also act as a fail-safe – making sure you take the right jobs and leave the wrong ones alone.

Targeting benchmarks can be broken down as follows:

- **The job** This should be the easy part. What are you seeking to gain from your job hunting? Is it promotion, for example? If so, what's the next job up the ladder?
- **The pay** More pay is often the reason why people look for another job. Pay is tricky and this is why we will deal with it separately (keep reading).
- **The area** How mobile you are clearly has a bearing on the kind of jobs you will be applying for. For example, are you a truly global person who is happy to work anywhere in the world or, at the other end of the scale, do your partner's job and/or family commitments tie you to looking for work within commuting distance of where you live now?
- **The risk** Would you only be interested in a secure job with a big-name employer or would you be happy to entertain something with a little more risk attached to it (e.g. a start-up business)? Again, a lot here will depend on your domestic situation. Are you the sole breadwinner for your family, for example? Or does your partner have a secure, well-paid job, meaning, perhaps that you can afford to take a few risks?
- **The hours** Some jobs involve working strange or anti-social hours. How would you feel about this? Alternatively, are you just looking for something part-time or hours that fit round your other commitments?
- **The prospects** Are these important to you? If so, it will rule out any employers where the prospects are limited (e.g. very small firms in static- or low-growth situations).
- **Anything else?** What we're fishing for here is anything peculiar to you that will have a bearing on the kind of job you can go for. For example, do you have a medical problem that could preclude working in certain industries or environments? Alternatively, would your family circumstances make it difficult for you to have nights away from home?

Simple though it seems, this exercise in setting out your targeting benchmarks is what will give your job hunting the structure and direction it needs. Targeting, remember, is about being selective. This means that any job that falls short of your targeting benchmarks is a job you won't be applying for. Another way of looking at this is: the more focused you are on the target, the more chances you have of hitting it.

WARNING!
Don't fall into the trap of scanning the ads and applying for jobs simply because they're there. If weeks go by without seeing a job that comes up to scratch, view it as evidence that your targeting is working.

The problem of pay

Pay, as we noted a few moments ago, is an awkward area mainly because a conflict can and does arise between:

* your estimation of your own worth, *and*
* what the market is capable of offering at any one given point.

One of the bigger problems here is that, at the outset of job hunting, you will have little or no idea of what the market can provide – in short, whether the kind of figures you have in mind are going over the top, not enough or somewhere in between.

Sources of information on rates of pay

When setting your pay targeting benchmark, try tapping into three sources:

1 **the visible market** – the jobs you see advertised in newspapers, journals or on websites (jobs which call for people with similar skills and experience to yours)
2 **your networks** – contacts in your profession who may be able to give you some valuable inside information on what other employers pay

3 **recruitment professionals** – somewhere along the line you will be talking to people like recruitment consultants, people whose job it is to know about going rates.

From these sources you will be able to form a quick overview of whether the figure you have in mind is realizable or not. Incidentally, don't rule out the possibility of finding out that you're not so badly paid after all – meaning:

● if your only reason for changing jobs is more money, you may want to think again
● if your problem is something other than money (e.g. security, lack of prospects), you may have to contemplate stepping sideways pay-wise – or even backwards.

Fine-tuning your pay targeting benchmark

Fine-tuning your pay targeting benchmark is something you do in the light of experience. For example, if the feedback you get from your job hunting suggests you may be asking for too much, then be ready to do one of the following:

● tweak your benchmark down a few notches
● stick with your original benchmark but realize that you're targeting just a narrow segment of well-paid jobs (top-end targeting)
● call off your job hunting altogether.

Targeting and accessibility

If you go back to yesterday's lesson, you will remember the point we made about making employers aware of exactly where you're coming from and what you're seeking to achieve. You will remember also that the main vehicle for this transparency and accessibility is your CV.

A common misunderstanding of the purpose of a CV is to see it only as the means of getting you interviews. While this is important, it is equally important that your CV conveys enough about you and your ambitions to enable employers to spot any mismatches between what you want and what they've got to offer. Don't, therefore, be tempted to use your CV to pull the wool over people's eyes. Present yourself exactly as you are and help employers to make the judgement as to whether the job is right for you or not. Getting interviews is no good if the jobs are time-wasters.

Summary

As you have found out today, targeting is not just something you do at the start of your expedition into the job jungle. Rather, it is something that you keep doing as you go along. You keep adjusting the compass bearings. You learn from every job application you make. You listen to the feedback you get from every interview you go to. You listen to what people like recruitment consultants tell you. You pick the brains of colleagues who have been active on the job market recently.

From all these sources you put together a picture and you keep comparing the picture with the targeting benchmarks you have drawn up. If you see the benchmarks diverging from what you see in the picture, then it is time to take stock.

Here, always be prepared to be flexible and do not fall into the trap of setting your ideas in cement. Ideas get better if you give them a chance to develop, whereas fixed ideas can and do have a tendency to veer away from reality. Sooner than you know it, you are back to those jobs that you can't do or that don't exist.

SUNDAY
MONDAY
TUESDAY
WEDNESDAY
THURSDAY
FRIDAY
SATURDAY

Fact-check (answers at the back)

1. How should you measure the success of your job hunting?
   a) By the number of applications you make ☐
   b) By the number of interviews you get ☐
   c) By the number of jobs you are offered ☐
   d) By the number of jobs you are offered that match up to your targeting benchmarks ☐

2. You go for an interview and the interviewer tells you that you do not have enough experience. Two weeks later you see a similar job advertised with a different employer. Do you...
   a) Apply? ☐
   b) See applying as a waste of time? ☐
   c) Apply, see if you get an interview, then see what feedback you get this time? ☐
   d) Phone up before you apply, tell them about your experience and ask them what chance you stand of getting the job? ☐

3. What is the purpose of a CV?
   a) To get you interviews ☐
   b) To get you interviews that aren't time wasters ☐
   c) To show you are professional ☐
   d) To make you look better than you really are ☐

4. You see a great job advertised where you do not have all the qualifications. Do you...
   a) Apply, tell the truth and let the employer decide whether you can do the job or not? ☐
   b) Give the job a miss? ☐
   c) Use a bit of spin? ☐
   d) Say you have got all the qualifications (i.e. tell a lie)? ☐

5. You have been for a lot of interviews but the salaries on offer never match up to your expectations. Do you...
   a) Adjust your targeting benchmarks? ☐
   b) Check your CV and make sure your pay expectations are clearly flagged up? ☐
   c) Do nothing (carry on with your applications)? ☐
   d) Blame employers for paying poor salaries? ☐

6. You want to find out if your pay expectations are realistic. Which of these sources will give you the best information?
   a) Recruitment consultants ☐
   b) Your human resources manager ☐
   c) Salary surveys ☐
   d) The Internet ☐

7. Jobs in start-up businesses are too risky. Do you...
   a) Agree? ☐
   b) Disagree? ☐
   c) Feel the answer depends on your personal circumstances? ☐
   d) Hold no opinion? ☐

SUNDAY MONDAY TUESDAY WEDNESDAY THURSDAY FRIDAY SATURDAY

8. You have been looking for a job for 12 months but so far you have only found two that match up with your targeting benchmarks. To find out where you may be going wrong, what do you look at first?
a) Your sourcing ☐
b) Your targeting ☐
c) Your accessibility ☐
d) Your application ☐

9. You are doing everything right but you are still getting asked to interviews that are time-wasters. What do you do?
a) Ring up each time and ask for more information over the phone ☐
b) Accept that sometimes this happens ☐
c) Take a break from job hunting ☐
d) Give the interviewers a piece of your mind ☐

10. Which of these is a sign that your targeting is going wrong?
a) Getting on shortlists every time and then finding the job is offered to someone else ☐
b) Applying for jobs and getting no interviews ☐
c) Getting interviews and then finding the jobs are not suitable ☐
d) Not getting replies to your applications ☐

SUNDAY
MONDAY
TUESDAY
WEDNESDAY
THURSDAY
FRIDAY
SATURDAY

WEDNESDAY

Attacking the visible market

Today you'll learn about applying for jobs on the visible market – the jobs that are advertised and (if the jobs are good jobs) the jobs that are going to attract other applicants in large numbers.

On Sunday we introduced you to the term 'reactive sourcing'. Reactive sourcing is what you do when you want to engage the visible market. It consists largely of keeping your eyes open and looking in the right places, notably at newspapers, journals and periodicals and on websites.

In this chapter we will look at these sources of visible market jobs in more detail and bring into play what you taught yourself yesterday about targeting and being selective when it comes to choosing which jobs to apply for.

Today you'll learn how to engage and see off competition, because the first task you face on the visible market is to make sure that your application stands out from the rest. Take it as read that the crowd will be there, but by the end of today you will know what to do to make sure that you are at the front of the queue and that you don't get ignored in the crush.

Sources of visible market jobs

Reactive sourcing is the term that describes the way in which you engage the visible market.

Reactive sourcing, remember, is where the stimulus is provided by the employer – usually in the form of advertising. How you respond to this stimulus determines how effective you are in engaging the visible market.

For convenience we've broken down sources of visible market jobs into the following:

- ads in newspapers and journals
- the Internet
- other sources.

Ads in newspapers and journals

Advertising in newspapers and journals is still one of the most popular ways of recruiting people. 'Scanning the ads' is, therefore, an important part of job hunting. It is where most of us start out on our search for a new job.

The choice of **newspapers** can be baffling and, with job hunting in mind, it is sometimes difficult to know which ones to take:

- **Local papers:** These vary quite a lot in the quality of the recruitment advertising they carry but, on the whole, they are essential reading from the job hunter's point of view. Local papers frequently have 'jobs nights' or nights on which they feature jobs in certain fields (e.g. engineering and technical appointments).

● **National papers:** Some national papers have strong toe-holds in certain sectors of the market. Other than this, 'pick 'n' mix' your choice of national papers and ring the changes from time to time. The same goes for Sunday papers. Because of the cost, broadsheets tend to carry advertising for top jobs only.

TIP **WARNING!**
Don't try and scan the ads in every newspaper. You haven't got the time.

Journals and periodicals that carry recruitment advertising divide into two types:

1 journals published by professional associations
2 trade journals of the kind that circulate in certain industries.

> ## Verdict on journals
>
> Good points: well targeted job wise (some journals put out by professional associations are regarded as top sources of jobs in their particular fields).
>
> Bad points: tend to be national or international publications, meaning that the jobs will be 'anywhere and everywhere' (a less attractive feature for those who are targeting jobs in specific areas).

The Internet

More and more employers use their websites for sourcing staff – indeed, the day may come when all recruitment is done online.
   Recruitment websites divide into two types:

1 sites run by recruitment specialists
2 employers' sites – organizations using their own websites to advertise vacancies.

Employers do not always use their own websites to advertise vacancies (some do, some don't). Don't, therefore, rely on them it exclusively – as some job hunters have been tempted to do. See it, instead, as yet another way of accessing the visible market. In other words, see it as complementing your other methods of reactive sourcing.

Other sources

Advertising on the radio, advertising on electronic billboards sited in public places, advertising in newsletters put out by the local branches of professional associations – the methods employers use to attract applicants are almost endless. The message is: keep your eyes and ears open.

Deciding which jobs to go for

With any job you source, the first decision you have to make is whether to apply for it or not. Here is where you go back to your targeting benchmarks. Does the job match up to your specification or doesn't it? If it does, then the green light is flashing at you to get moving. If not, an equally strong signal should be beaming out to you to go no further.

TIP

WARNING!
Never view it as a foregone conclusion that you will be applying for every job you source – indeed, applying for the wrong jobs is fraught with all kinds of dangers:

- *You can find yourself squandering precious time off work on pointless interviews.*

- *Employers can usually spot square pegs, so wrong jobs tend to be jobs you don't get – chalking up turndowns like this leads to discouragement.*

- *The experience will be misleading – for example, if you apply for a lot of poorly paid jobs you will form the impression (wrongly) that the poor level of pay is the norm.*

Worst of all, you could find yourself in the wrong job.

Advertisements without salaries

Being selective about the jobs you apply for by running them across your targeting benchmarks is all well and good, but a problem you frequently have to face up to is the ad that makes no mention of salary other than the meaningless jumble of words such as 'negotiable' or 'commensurate with the responsibilities'. The job looks OK but, without any insight into the pay, how do you know whether it's worth applying for or not?

As we all know, pay is a difficult area shrouded in mists of secrecy. Why don't employers put salaries in ads? In most cases, the reason will be one of the following:

- confidentiality (not wanting the world at large to know what salaries they pay)
- their salaries are poor and they don't like to say
- they're fishing (they want to see what you're earning first so they can decide whether they can afford you or not).

So how do you deal with ads with no salaries? On the face of it, the sensible approach to the problem seems to be to ring up and ask. You don't want to waste anyone's time so, before you put an application in, could they give you a rough idea of the kind of figure they have in mind please? Sensible though it sounds, anecdotal evidence of this approach actually working is rather thin on the ground. Often all you get is a lot of cagey answers that don't move you forward very far.

Make your pay expectations accessible

Going back to Monday's lesson, we stressed the importance of always making it crystal clear to employers exactly where you are coming from and what you are seeking to achieve. In the case of pay, this means two things:

1 your current earnings
2 the level of earnings you're aspiring to.

This information is what needs to figure prominently in your CV and mentioned again in any letters of application you send in. Because of the secretiveness and sensitivity that surrounds pay and because of the special problems arising from ads without salaries, this kind of accessibility acts as a fail-safe to ensure that your application goes no further if the employer's ideas on pay don't fall into line with your own. In short, deal with ads with no pay as follows:

● check first of all to make sure all your other targeting benchmarks are met
● revisit your CV and satisfy yourself that no one reading it will get any wrong ideas about your pay aspirations
● put together an equally accessible accompanying letter
● send off your application and see what happens.

Conditioning your expectations

There is a snag with the above approach and it is this. Not many employers will own up to not being able to afford you so the likely response if the pay available falls way below your targeting benchmark is a standard 'sorry but no thank you' letter. Since 'sorry and no thank you' letters are a source of discouragement, when replying to ads with no salaries you need to condition your expectations accordingly. If you get turned down, tell yourself it's an even chance that the job's to blame – not you. This is all part of getting your expectations into line that we talked about yesterday under the subject of application.

Read advertisements properly

Ensuring that jobs match up to your targeting benchmarks sounds easy enough so why is it that so many people get it wrong? The reason in a lot of cases is not reading the ad properly or, rather, reading it selectively so that, consciously or not, we ignore:

● any stipulations that render us unsuitable – e.g. 'candidates must be able to converse fluently in Mandarin Chinese'
● job conditions that come into conflict with our targeting benchmarks, e.g. 'the work can involve anti-social hours including weekends'.

This blanking out of things we don't want to see usually happens when the job is a good job – typically one where a good salary is on offer. In the excitement to get an application off, we omit to go through the small print in too much detail or we see the bit that jars in our minds but decide to give it a whirl anyway.

Read job ads carefully. Employers usually go to a lot of trouble to draft the copy so that unsuitable candidates aren't drawn into applying. They are as concerned as you are that no one's time is wasted.

Dealing with competition

Engaging the visible market means facing up to competition. The amount of competition you have to deal with depends on two things:

1 how good the job is
2 how widely it has been advertised.

Where there is a lot of competition, being suitable for a job is no guarantee that you will get an interview. What you also need to ensure is that:

- your suitability comes across in one quick read of your CV (your *accessibility*)
- you can be contacted without any fuss and bother, plus the fact you can come in for interviews quickly (your *availability*)
- any strong points you have are brought into prominence (your super *accessibility*).

We dealt with the first two of these bullet points on Monday. Now let's look at the third.

Bringing out your strong points

Strong points mean your strong points vis-à-vis a particular job application. What this doesn't mean is what you see as your strong points generally. For example, you may have had a lot of very interesting experience with a certain brand of computer-aided design software but this won't cut much ice at all with an employer who uses a completely different package. The point here is to get you to see each job application as a fresh challenge. There will be more on this as we move on.

Strong points are the matches between what the employer is looking for and what you have to offer. A strong point could be the fact that you hold a particular qualification. Alternatively, it could be your experience with a certain technique or that living out of a suitcase for months on end is something you're completely used to. The clues to these matches can be found in the ad itself – in what employers have to say about themselves and in what they see as desirable attributes in candidates (another good reason for making sure you read ads properly).

Bringing your strong points into prominence

At the application stage you normally have three ways of bringing your strong points to the attention of an employer:

1 in your CV
2 in any supporting letters you submit
3 in any application forms you fill in.

● **Use their words:** This is one of the golden rules to getting across your strong points. In a world where there is an ever-increasing use of buzz words and jargon, a very real danger exists of the strong point you're trying to bring out falling on stony ground because it isn't understood or fully appreciated. The way to avoid this difficulty is by putting your own preferences to one side and always using the same buzz words and jargon as the employer (the same words as those used in the ad).

CV scanning software

- Preliminary scanning of CVs is sometimes done by computer, meaning that your application could end up in the turn-down pile without it ever having been seen by human eyes. What CV scanning software is programmed to do is search for key matches between what appears in your CV and the specification for the job. It does this by identifying certain key words and phrases – all of which lends a new importance to the choice of terminology you use.

- **Customizing your CV:** This should present no problems if you keep a copy of your CV stored on disk or a memory stick. Simply get it up on screen and edit it. What you are seeking to achieve here is to bring your strong points into prominence without breaking the rule about keeping your CV short and concise. Be warned, however, this may mean taking out some cherished piece of information to make the necessary space. Console yourself with the fact that the strong point will have more bearing on whether you get picked for an interview or not.
- **Accompanying letters:** The letter you send in accompanying your CV is another place to get across your strong points. Don't worry about repeating what's already in your CV.
- **Application forms:** Most larger firms have standard application forms and there's a fair chance you could be asked to complete one at the early stages of an application, i.e. before you know whether you've been granted an interview or not. Application forms usually have a section headed: 'Any other information you wish to add in support of your application.' Use sections like these to list your strong points.

TIP ··

WARNING!

As a general rule people give insufficient attention to filling in application forms. They dash them off quickly and this is a mistake. Remember next time you fill in an application form that it will probably get a better reading than the CV you spent hours preparing.

··

Follow the instructions

In the tailpiece to every ad you will find instructions on how to apply. These instructions usually include:

● the name and/or job title of the person to whom your application should be sent
● the form in which the application should be submitted, e.g. a current CV together with an accompanying letter
● any references you should quote
● any closing date for applications
● how your application should be submitted – by post, fax, or email, or you may have to ring and ask for an application form to be sent to you.

What is important about these instructions is that you follow them to the letter and that you don't substitute your own ideas on 'what's best'. With large numbers of applicants and employers recruiting for more than one position at the same time, there is

always the danger of individual applications getting mislaid or put on the wrong pile. Needless to say, you won't make a very good job of engaging the competition if you're not there to do it.

Don't procrastinate

Even though there may be no mention of a closing date for applications, don't let the grass grow under your feet when you're attacking the visible market. Remember, the world won't wait while you're finding the time to put the finishing touches to your CV or other distractions seem more pressing.

Application, the third of our three As, is the watchword here. Get moving.

Selection consultants

Finally, today, a passing acknowledgement of the fact that a lot of visible market jobs are advertised by firms of selection consultants. This reflects one or both of the following:

● the need for the employer's identity to remain confidential (not necessarily evidence that someone is about to get the sack),
● the need for expertise of the kind the employer doesn't have (expertise the selection consultants can offer).

With advertisements placed by selection consultants, is there a danger you could find yourself applying for your own job?

While this may be an extremely remote prospect, what is more worrying perhaps is that the application you sent off to Boggis & Associates, Selection Consultants, could somehow find its way into the wrong hands – namely the hands of your boss. Not knowing the identity of the employer behind the ad is a real area of concern for a lot of people. Could it be, for example, a company that is in the same group as your own?

Firms of selection consultants sometimes offer a confidential reply service meaning you can list out the names of any employers you don't want your details sent to. Failing this, ring the consultants up and ask them how else they can address your concerns. If you're still left feeling uneasy then it may be best to give the job a miss. When job hunting, your first priority always is to look after the job you've got and never to put it at risk.

Summary

Today you have learned the importance of being selective when it comes to applying for jobs that have been advertised. Yes, the jobs are there but because they are there does not necessarily mean you should be writing off for them. See first of all that they measure up to your targeting benchmarks. If they do, great; but, if they do not, then stick to your benchmarks and give them a miss. Remember: with job hunting you do not measure your performance by the count of applications you have sent off.

Today you have also taught yourself not to be put off when you know that you will be up against stiff competition. Take competition as read when you apply for any good job that has been advertised but, rather than occupying your mind with negative thoughts like 'What chance do I stand?', turn your attention instead to what matters – seeing what's good about your application and, more importantly still, seeing what steps you should be taking to make sure everyone knows what's good. In other words, let the need to engage and overcome competition stimulate you into giving your application your best shot.

SUNDAY

MONDAY

TUESDAY

WEDNESDAY

THURSDAY

FRIDAY

SATURDAY

Fact-check (answers at the back)

1. You see a good job advertised but you are concerned that there could be hundreds of applicants. Do you...
   a) Apply? ❏
   b) Feel you stand no chance and give the job a miss? ❏
   c) Hand-deliver your application so it gets in first? ❏
   d) Ring up and ask the employer how many applications they have received? ❏

2. A job that interests you is advertised but the salary indicated is £10k under the figure you are looking for. Do you...
   a) Apply and hope you get an interview where you can negotiate the salary? ❏
   b) Flag up your pay requirements in your application? ❏
   c) Give the job a miss? ❏
   d) Ring up first and try to negotiate a higher salary over the phone? ❏

3. You see an ad for a job but there is no mention of salary. Your main reason for looking for another job is so that you can better your pay. Do you...
   a) Give the job a miss? ❏
   b) Ring up and ask the employer to tell you the salary? ❏
   c) Apply and hope for the best? ❏
   d) Apply but make sure that your pay requirements are made clear in your application? ❏

4. What are your strong points?
   a) Points about you that make matches with the requirements of the job ❏
   b) Areas where you have had most experience ❏
   c) Your outstanding achievements ❏
   d) Your academic qualifications ❏

5. You are asked to fill an application form in and see a box headed 'Any additional information'. What do you put in this box?
   a) Nothing (leave it blank) ❏
   b) Your strong points ❏
   c) That you work hard ❏
   d) What your boss said to you at your last appraisal interview ❏

6. You are asked to fill in an application form and see straight away that most of the information requested is a repeat of the information in your CV. You have already submitted a CV, so do you...
   a) Ring up and query why you are being asked to provide the same information twice? ❏
   b) Send in another copy of your CV and write 'see CV' in the spaces on the form? ❏
   c) Fill in the form and send it back? ❏
   d) Send in another copy of your CV and ignore the form? ❏

7. You see a job advertised by a firm of consultants where the identity of the employer is not revealed. You are concerned that the job could be with a company in the same group as your current employer. You do not want it to get back to your boss that you are looking for another job. Do you...

a) Give the job a miss? ❏
b) Ring the consultants, ask them to reveal the name of the employer, and give the job a miss if they refuse? ❏
c) Ring up the consultants, explain the problem and see if they come up with an answer? ❏
d) Apply and not worry about it? ❏

8. You see a great job advertised where applicants are invited to send in a CV. You realize that your CV needs updating but you are pushed for time. What do you do?

a) Burn the midnight oil ❏
b) Send in your CV as it stands ❏
c) Ring the employer, explain the problem and find out if they will hold the job open for a few weeks ❏
d) Update your CV and send it in late ❏

9. You see a job advertised but you know that there will be hundreds of applicants. Which of the following will help you to get an interview?

a) Ring up and say you will only apply if you are given an interview ❏
b) Take in your application in person and ask someone to see you ❏
c) Send in your application then ring up a few days later and ask to book an interview ❏
d) None of the above ❏

10. You see a job advertised on an employer's website but when you apply you get an email back saying the job was filled some time ago. Do you...

a) Email a reply to tell them to update their website? ❏
b) As a), but add on a complaint that your time has been wasted by their inefficiency? ❏
c) Do nothing but make a note never to apply for any more jobs with this employer? ❏
d) Do nothing and accept that web sites are not always updated when they should be? ❏

SUNDAY

MONDAY

TUESDAY

WEDNESDAY

THURSDAY

FRIDAY

SATURDAY

THURSDAY

Attacking the elusive invisible market

Today you will learn all you need to know about accessing jobs on the invisible market:

- the jobs that are not advertised
- the jobs that employers keep to themselves
- the jobs that are rumoured to be the best jobs.

Perhaps the most striking feature of the invisible market is its sheer size. Although there is no accurate count of how many jobs are filled without advertising, a conservative estimate would be around 90 per cent. In other words, the invisible market is far, far bigger than its visible counterpart and aspiring job hunters should not let this fact escape them. Furthermore, competition is rarely an issue. Because the jobs have not been advertised, it is unusual to find more than a handful of applicants for each one. In fact, there is a good chance of you finding yourself in the enviable position of being the only face in the frame.

So today you'll learn how to set about accessing the elusive invisible market – what you have to do and how you need to go about approaching employers if you want to prise out what they have chosen to keep under wraps.

Why the invisible market exists

Going back to Sunday's lesson, we picked out a number of reasons for the growth of the invisible market. Let's now extend this list to give you a complete appreciation of why the invisible market exists:

- the cost of advertising – laying out large sums of money with no guarantee that the outcome will be successful
- the resources and expertise needed to deal with response to advertisements – resources and expertise employers may not have
- the fear of making bad selection decisions coupled with the increased prospect of employers have to face litigation from people they have sacked
- the impact of skills shortages on recruitment
- the commonly held view that 'advertising doesn't work'
- bad experiences with advertising – a double whammy when the cost is also taken into account
- employers in a hurry – in a technology-driven age, the tendency for anything slow and ponderous to be viewed as intrinsically bad.

Invisible market methods

Against this background, more and more employers are turning to alternative methods of recruitment, notably:

- recruitment consultants (agencies) – people who are usually prepared to work on a 'no placement, no fee' basis and can put up shortlists of candidates at 24 to 48 hours' notice
- contacts – putting the word round in the trade or to selected individuals (e.g. people who work for competitors)
- revisiting CVs that are held on file
- using headhunters.

Accessing the invisible market

Let's now look at what you need to do to access this vibrant and expanding invisible market.

> Remember proactive sourcing? Proactive sourcing is the key to getting to know about jobs that aren't advertised. Proactive sourcing is where you provide the stimulus.

Cold calling

This is one very obvious way of finding out if employers have got any vacancies that they're not telling the world about – simply by ringing up and asking them.

There is a right and a wrong way to go about cold calling. The wrong way is to ring an employer once, leave your name, phone number and a few personal details, then leave it to chance they'll remember you the next time a suitable vacancy comes up.

At best, a cold call reveals a snapshot of what's available in an organization at a particular point in time. Expect no more from it and you won't be disappointed. For instance, the chances of the person you spoke to remembering you in three months' time when a vacancy comes up are extremely remote. The scrap of paper where he/she wrote down your name will have disappeared a long time ago.

A model approach to cold calling

Done systematically, cold calling can be a very effective way of accessing the invisible market. Here is what to do:

- Start by picking **the right employers** – organizations that are likely to have the kind of job opportunities you are targeting. To an extent, this is inspired guesswork but clues to suitable employers can sometimes be picked up from reading the job ads (e.g. companies who are doing a lot of recruiting).

- Get **the name of the right person** to speak to – e.g. if you're an accountant, ask for the name of the financial manager. Don't be fobbed off here with the name of the personnel or human resources manager – even though they may be the normal channel that applicants go through.

- **Keep it brief.** Remember, cold calls can be irritating, especially to someone who is busy. State simply who you are, what you're looking for and whether there's anything suitable for you at the moment.

- If you strike lucky, **keep the momentum going.** Suggest an interview and get in quickly – i.e. use your *availability* to maximum effect. Alternatively, if you find there's nothing doing, then, consistent with not outstaying your welcome, find out if the organization ever has the kind of job opportunities you are targeting. This, if you like, is your market research.

- End the call by **saying thank you.** Leave the door open for calling again another time.

- **Keep a record** of your calls including the name of the person to whom you spoke and any useful information you picked up.

- **Give each call a score from 0 to 5.** Your 5s will be calls where the feedback has been encouraging (employers who are worth keeping in touch with regularly). Your 2s and 3s will be those who only have an occasional demand for talents such as yours. Give zero scores to employers who give you a hard time. Don't waste any more effort on them.

- **Work out a call cycle.** For example, put your 5s down for a call every two months or so, whereas your 2s and 3s won't need to be contacted quite so frequently.

- **Stand by to revise your ratings** (upwards or downwards) – each call reveals a little bit more of the picture.

TIP

WARNING!
Cold calling companies too frequently achieves little – the snapshot is still the same and you run the risk of getting yourself viewed as a pest.

Systematic and targeted cold calling eventually pays off. As the number of companies on your call list diminishes, the target will become more accurate and defined. Sooner or later statistical probability takes over from pure chance and you start to connect with good jobs. Patience and persistence are the watchwords here (all part of *application*).

Cold calling is a good way of getting to know about vacancies before they're advertised or put out to recruitment consultants – a case of getting in before the competition arrives.

Mailshots

Sending your CV off to prospective employers is another way of accessing the invisible market. Again, there's a right and a wrong way of going about it:

- **Don't expect a reply:** Whether employers should acknowledge every unsolicited CV they receive is a matter of opinion. The fact that many of them don't is, however, something you are going to have to learn to live with – a point we have touched on already.

- **Focus on the aim:** Rather than getting wound up about matters of no importance, such as how many standard letters of acknowledgement you do or don't notch up, concentrate instead on what really matters, which is:
  - that your mailshots may strike lucky and land on the right desk at the right time
  - failing this, that your mailshots have enough impact to ensure that they get put on the right file (the one revisited whenever vacancies for people like you come up).
- **Redesigning your CV:** Yesterday, when we looked at attacking the visible market, we placed great emphasis on customizing your CV and, in particular, on setting out your strong points vis-à-vis each application. With the invisible market, this isn't quite so easy because there isn't an advertisement to look at for clues on what to put in and what to leave out. The answer? Use your imagination and try to customize each unsolicited CV you send out to what you think the employer will be looking for.

Example

If you're seeking a position in general management and you're mailshotting a small firm, perhaps you need to bring out your experience in managing small teams or your hands-on approach or your good all-round business skills. Conversely, the experience you've had running multi-site operations won't have too much relevance and should therefore be relegated to a less prominent place.

Here are two important points about customizing CVs:

1 Print off a second copy (one you can keep on file so you will have a record of what you've said to a particular target if you're invited for an interview).
2 Don't neglect to do it, and take some time over it, because employers receive hundreds of unsolicited CVs and they automatically bin those that don't strike immediate chords with them.

A model approach to mailshots

If you want mailshots to work for you, this is what you need to do:

- Again, identify **the right employers** – employers who are likely to have the kind of opportunities that match your targeting.

- **Ring before putting anything in the post.** The object of this exercise is to get the name of the person in the organization who would be responsible for employing people like you, i.e. the decision maker. Again, don't be fobbed off with the name of the human resources manager. Human resources managers aren't decision makers (unless you happen to be looking for a job in human resources, of course).

- **Put an accompanying letter with your CV.** Keep this short and simple: who you are, where you're coming from and what you're seeking to achieve. Let it serve as an appetizser for the main meal (your CV).

- **Mark your envelope 'Confidential'.** This is the best insurance you can give your CV that it will be read by the right pair of eyes.

Fax shots and emails

An alternative to putting your CV in the post is to fax it or send it by email. What's best?

Go back to your aims. Once your CV has passed through the preliminary read test and, given there are no suitable vacancies at the moment, what you want to ensure is that:

● your CV is put on file,
● when it is retrieved from file, it will still be in more or less pristine condition.

On the second count, faxes don't acquit themselves too well, while, with emails, there is always the risk they don't get printed off – meaning that they fail on the first count. At risk of sounding prehistoric, therefore – and unless there are any overriding reasons for doing otherwise – put your unsolicited CV in the post.

Post or email?

A CV submitted by email would seem to win hands down where it is the practice to store details of interesting-looking candidates on an **electronic database.** One of the problems facing you, however, is knowing which employers do this and which don't. Since you will be sending your CV to individual named managers rather than to the Human Resources or the Personnel Department (where these computer-based systems tend to be located), the advice to 'put it in the post' still holds good.

Putting your speculative CVs in the post as opposed to faxing them or sending them by email is a good example of **keeping control** – playing an active rather than a passive role in ensuring your job hunting moves to successful conclusions; facilitating the process as far as you can rather than leaving it to chance or how some hard-pressed manager happens to feel inclined on the day. Keeping control has particular importance when accessing the invisible market. We shall see more of it as we move on.

Professional networking

Professional networking is another way of accessing the invisible market – using your circle of contacts in business as a source of suitable job opportunities – something most people only think to do when they're out of work or their jobs come under threat.

Did you know?
More people find jobs by professional networking than by any other method.

Networking is for everyone

A common misconception of networking is that it is the preserve of social climbers or extrovert personality types. Nothing could be further from the truth. Anyone in a career has his or her own professional network. Typically it consists of:

- work colleagues past and present – bosses, peers and subordinates
- other people you come into contact with in the course of your work – for example, customers, suppliers, outside service providers
- people you know through your professional body, e.g. the local branch of the Institute of Management
- people you meet through going on courses or while getting qualifications – people in similar lines of work to yourself.

WARNING!
*With the relatively small worlds that most of us operate in, sourcing jobs by professional networking carries the risk of our job hunting ambitions reaching the **wrong ears**. Take the case of Leonard. Leonard is a sales manager in the telecommunications industry. Leonard tried tapping into his contacts in the competition to see what jobs might be available but unfortunately his boss got to hear about it. The result? Leonard was in very deep trouble indeed.*

A model approach to networking for jobs

The key to networking for jobs successfully
is keeping control:

• **Don't use your network contacts as
sounding boards** for your grouses and groans. It
will feed out entirely the wrong messages – i.e.
that you're only looking for an escape route from your
present difficulties and any job will do.

• Instead, make sure that the messages you feed out to
your network contacts are **complete messages.**
Give precise guidelines on the kind of job you're
looking for – including the salary.

• **Set the parameters** by telling your contacts
how far you want them to go for you. This would
normally be to effect an introduction. In other words,
you should make it clear that you want any detailed
negotiations left to you (always better done first hand).

• **Stress the importance of confidentiality**.
Lay down precise rules – like you want no discussions
with any third parties without your prior knowledge
and consent.

The lesson here is only to network with people you can trust – people you can rely on to look after your best interests and who won't compromise your position by indulging in tittle-tattle. Conversely, give a wide berth to those who don't meet these criteria.

Registering with recruitment consultants

A large slice of the invisible market is handled by firms of recruitment consultants (employment agencies). Recruitment consultants keep details of candidates on file and interested employers can access these details at short notice. Here are examples of two employers who chose to use recruitment consultants for different reasons:

Example – Company D

Company D's IT Manager unexpectedly handed in her notice halfway through a major project. With no suitable internal candidates to promote, Company D was faced with having to recruit someone from outside. The rigmarole of placing advertisements didn't appeal to Company D mainly because of the time it would take. Company D decided, therefore, to run their vacancy through a couple of firms of recruitment consultants specializing in IT staff to see if they had anybody on their books who would fit the bill.

Example – Company E

Company E's recently promoted Chief Accountant proved to be a total failure and they decided that he would have to go back to his old job at some stage in the near future. Before they broached this subject with him, however, they felt they needed to know if anyone more suitable was available on the market. A quick and confidential way of checking this out was to ask a leading firm of financial recruitment consultants to send in details of candidates they had registered with them.

No placement, no fee

Other than quickness, most firms of recruitment consultants offer their services on a no placement, no fee basis. This means employers like Company D and Company E can have a look at who's available without it costing them anything.

Choose the right consultants

In picking firms of recruitment consultants to register with, you will normally find you are faced with a bewildering choice. You need to apply the following criteria:

- The consultants must deal with the kind of appointments you are targeting. For example, if you're looking for a management position in the construction industry, it is pointless registering with a firm of consultants who deal mainly in general office staff.
- They need to be effective, which is, in part, a reflection of their client base and, in part, a reflection of their general efficiency. (With firms of recruitment consultants, effectiveness should never be taken for granted!)

To go about finding the right firm of recruitment consultants for your needs, first look at their website to check that they deal with the right types of job. Then conduct further research in the following way.

- **Seek personal recommendations** – for example, does anyone on your professional network have any recent experience of dealing with a firm of recruitment consultants? If so, what information can they pass on?
- **Check the business telephone directories** – recruitment consultants often have display entries telling you what they do.
- **Scan the job ads** – recruitment consultants frequently run advertisements for vacancies that have been notified to them. From reading these advertisements over a period of time it is possible to tell which consultants are active in the areas of the job market you are targeting.
- **Ask** – if in any doubt, ring up firms of consultants, give them a brief run-down of the kind of job you're looking for and ask if they can help.

> **TIP** ···
>
> **WARNING!**
>
> *Don't register with too many consultants because it can give you two problems:*
>
> 1 *too many requests to go to interviews (more than your availability will stand)*
>
> 2 *two or more firms of consultants putting you forward for the same job (this can queer the pitch before you even start).*
> ··

Registering with consultants

Registering usually involves filling in a registration form, sometimes attending an interview and sometimes doing some kind of test. Some firms of consultants offer the facility to register online. Once you have registered with a firm of consultants they will be able to use their contacts and know how to find you the kind of job you are seeking.

Keeping control

Those magic words again! Keeping control is the secret of success in dealing with recruitment consultants. Keeping control means:

- Make sure at the outset that they understand where you're coming from, i.e. go to great pains to explain your targeting, benchmarks and leave no room for doubt.

- Make sure that they know how to get hold of you. Recruitment consultants live in a fast-moving world where they have to get results both for their clients and for themselves (a lot of them are paid on commission). Needless to say, candidates they find hard to contact don't appeal to recruitment consultants one bit.
- Phone up or email consultants from time to time to find out how they are getting on. Not only will it remind them that you're still there but you might also pick up some interesting feedback (for example that the salary you're asking for is too high). Prick up your ears for feedback. Feedback, remember, is what you use to give your targeting benchmarks their fine-tuning.
- It's very important to advise consultants whenever any information they are holding on you changes, e.g. you get a new telephone number or you decide to tweak your pay targeting benchmark down a notch or two.
- Ditch any consultants who don't perform satisfactorily – especially consultants who waste your time by putting you forward for jobs that are completely wrong for you.

Summary

Today you have learned how to access the invisible job market using methods that fall under the heading of proactive sourcing – sourcing where the stimulus comes from you. You have seen at the same time how the invisible market operates, why it exists and the rewards that await you if you can succeed in engaging with it:

1 You will see what's really out there for you (the whole market as opposed to just the tiny slice of jobs that are advertised).

2 You will find that there is little or no competition on the invisible market.

3 As a consequence, you will find that there is more chance of you getting the jobs.

4 You will find more flexibility when it comes to negotiating terms such as salary and perks.

5 The big message about the invisible job market is not to be put off by its seeming impenetrability. It does call for application but the effort usually pays off.

SUNDAY
MONDAY
TUESDAY
WEDNESDAY
THURSDAY
FRIDAY
SATURDAY

Fact-check (answers at the back)

1. How do you access the invisible market?
a) By searching on the Internet ☐
b) By proactive sourcing ☐
c) By doing nothing ☐
d) Don't know ☐

2. Which of the following is proactive sourcing?
a) Sending out unsolicited CVs ☐
b) Searching for jobs advertised on the Internet ☐
c) Reading job ads in professional journals ☐
d) Scanning the job ads in local newspapers ☐

3. Who is it best to speak to when you call an employer to see if they have any suitable vacancies?
a) Whoever answers the phone ☐
b) The Managing Director ☐
c) The Human Resources Manager ☐
d) The manager responsible for the areas of the business where the jobs for people like you will be ☐

4. You cold call an employer but when you ask if there are any suitable vacancies you are told 'no'. Do you...
a) Strike them off your call list? ☐
b) Say you will send them a copy of your CV? ☐
c) Ask if they ever get vacancies for people like you and, if the answer is 'yes', say you will ring again? ☐
d) Ask if you can call round and see them? ☐

5. You send in an unsolicited CV and hear nothing. Do you...
a) Ring up and find out why? ☐
b) Put it down to bad manners? ☐
c) View the lack of response as normal? ☐
d) Write a letter of complaint to the Managing Director? ☐

6. You want to put out feelers to one of your firm's major competitors to see if they could offer you anything. Unfortunately, your only contact in the competitor's business is someone you do not trust. Do you...
a) Put your distrust to one side and put out the feeler anyway? ☐
b) Speak to someone else (someone you don't know)? ☐
c) Forget the idea? ☐
d) Get a friend to speak to them for you? ☐

7. One of the recruitment consultants you are registered with phones you up about a position with one of their clients. Unfortunately, the position is completely unsuitable. Do you...
a) Try explaining what you are looking for again and give them one last chance to get it right? ☐
b) Tell them to stop wasting your time? ☐
c) Take your name off their register (and say you want no more calls from them)? ☐
d) View the experience as being part of the price you have to pay for dealing with recruitment consultants? ☐

8. Two recruitment consultants phone you about what appears to be the same job. The job sounds great but do you...

a) Let both recruitment consultants put you forward and, by doing this, feel you will be doubling your chances of getting the job? ❏

b) Tell one consultant you are not interested to prevent any complications about who introduced you to the client first arising later on? ❏

c) Tell the two consultants to sort it out between themselves? ❏

d) Give the job a miss? ❏

9. How do most managers find positions?

a) By replying to ads in the press or on websites ❏

b) By going to consultants ❏

c) By professional networking ❏

d) By being headhunted ❏

10. What is the best way of submitting an unsolicited CV?

a) By email ❏

b) In the post ❏

c) By fax ❏

d) Delivering it by hand ❏

FRIDAY

Get
headhunted

Today you will learn how to get headhunted.

The world of executive search beckons where top appointments are filled by mysterious phone calls from complete strangers and over lunches in expensive restaurants – or so the story goes. But is there anything you can do to get your name on the headhunters' lists? Is it a matter of waiting for the approaches to come or can you exert any influence over the process?

By the end of today you will have a clear understanding of why the market for executive search exists and how it works. You will learn what headhunters are looking for and how they operate. You will see how important it is that you project an image that fits in with what headhunters want to see in the candidates they put forward to their clients.

Building on this understanding, you will then learn how to deal with headhunters and how it is possible to talk up items in the package such as salary and perks.

Finally, today you will learn what it takes to keep the approaches coming. Once you're on the headhunters' radar, what do you have to do to make sure you stay there?

The market for executive search

Executive search consultants don't come cheap, so the first point to grasp about headhunting is that employers don't go down this route unless there is a good reason. In most cases, the reason is that the job is a very senior job (e.g. a board-level appointment) where the person being sought is someone with exceptional qualities. Note: employers also use headhunting to recruit people with scarce and/or specialist skills.

What's in it for you?

Being headhunted is definitely something you can't afford to miss out on. There are two reasons for saying this:

1 many of the best jobs are filled by headhunting
2 the money's flexible (it's up to employers to come up with an offer that's going to interest you).

There are many things you can do to enhance your chances of being headhunted. Since headhunters work through their contacts, one of which might lead them to you, you will need to project a person-perfect and work-perfect image to everyone you know at all times, as if you were permanently at an interview.

How headhunters work

First, let's look at how headhunters work. Professional headhunters – or executive search consultants, as they are more properly known – thrive on their connections in the business world.

What the example of Company Q shows is that, to get yourself on to the receiving end of a headhunter's approach:

- someone has got to know you
- more importantly, what they know about you has got to be good.

Projecting the right image

For the most part, by 'people who know you' we mean people who have come into contact with you in the course of your work. This includes:

- colleagues, past and present (bosses, peers and subordinates)
- external contacts such as customers, suppliers and professional advisors
- people who know you through your work on outside bodies such as professional institutions and trade associations.

With being headhunted hot on the agenda, it is people like these who can influence the outcomes for you by:

● mentioning your name at the right moment,
● saying the right things about you.

This is where we ask you to focus your mind sharply on the image you project as you go about your day-to-day work.

The lifelong interview

An interesting contrast to draw here is between:

● the image you cultivate for going to interviews,
● the rather less well-managed image you project to those who have dealings with you every day of the week.

With the first, you are extremely mindful of being on your best behaviour while, at the same time, taking great pains over your personal appearance. You will be guarded in anything you say. You will certainly be going to great lengths to keep any grey areas in your track record under wraps.

Not so, however, with the second. You will be more inclined to let your hair down and a few of the less endearing aspects of your character may even creep out.

What we're talking about here, however, is about projecting an image *all of the time* rather than over the 45–90 minutes that's par for the course for most interviews. Harder? Of course it is – and this is what we mean by the lifelong interview. The consistency and application called for are not easy to achieve.

The lifelong interview in practice

- You don't have off days.

- You have to be 100-per-cent reliable – you get back to people when you say you will and you complete your work to targets.

- Your appearance is always up to scratch (don't be the first to dress down).

- You refrain from running down your colleagues and your bosses behind their backs – you keep your opinions on people to yourself.

- You don't whinge and whine – you don't use your colleagues as a sounding board for your grievances whenever you feel you're being given a hard time.

- You learn to keep your flaws to yourself.

- You give some of the gloss you save for interviews to every day.

TIP

WARNING!
Is there anything on the Internet (e.g. on a social networking site) that could put you in a bad light? If so, remove it.

Person perfect and work perfect

Headhunters get their business by reputation; hence they play safe when it comes to putting forward the names of candidates to their clients. Don't expect headhunters to be very interested in you, therefore, if:

- they know of any defects in your character, *and*
- your work record is not up to standard.

Rather, you must be seen as someone who is person perfect and work perfect and this is especially the case with top-drawer jobs.

Marketing yourself to headhunters

Headhunters have the reputation of being an aloof breed of
people who move in elitist social circles – inaccessible to the
Joe and Jane Ordinaries of this world. But is this true? Indeed,
are there ways of bringing your credentials to the attention of
headhunters so that you can enhance your chances of being
the target of an approach?

Don't pepper headhunters with CVs

First, there is a wrong way to go about it. Don't pepper headhunters
with copies of your CV – at least not until you've done some
groundwork first. Headhunters (proper ones) receive thousands of
unsolicited CVs. Most of them end up in the shredding machine.

Think about where headhunters are coming from

Ask yourself why a headhunter should be interested in you. What
do they stand to gain from having your name on their lists?

Headhunters are in business to make money – just like everyone
else. What plays the biggest part in how they view you is whether
they think they can make money out of you or not – in other words,
whether they could place you with one of their clients.

Identify unusual areas of skill and experience

Headhunting assignments frequently involve finding people
with unusual or special areas of skill and experience – people:

● who aren't in abundant supply, *and*
● whom advertising won't necessarily reach.

Example

Ask yourself if you've got any interesting areas of skill and experience. Take Garth as an example. Garth is the Financial Manager of a company that has recently gone through a major expansion programme. Garth, therefore, has a lot of knowledge of takeovers, mergers and acquisitions – a lot more than the average financial manager would have.

Use your connections

Play headhunters at their own game – by which we mean use your connections to access them. This is easy if you've been headhunted before. Speak to the consultant you dealt with previously and say you're ready to make another move. Explain what it is you're looking for this time.

A model approach to mailshots

• Use the phone for making contact.

• Quickly establish the connection: 'I got your name from Ruth Sykes. You placed her in a position with Wired Up Electronics six months ago.'

• Equally quickly, move on to where you're coming from and what you're seeking to achieve (your target). Do this in three sentences maximum.

• Mention any interesting areas of skill/experience (another sentence).

• Ask the headhunter if he/she can help you.

• Stop talking and listen to the answer.

If you're not fortunate enough to have been the target for an approach before, find someone among your circle who has. With search becoming an increasingly preferred method of sourcing executive talent, there is almost bound to be someone you know who has been the focus of a headhunter's attention at some point in the past. Find out from them the headhunter's name, then follow the plan of action set out above.

There are a number of possible outcomes here:

- The headhunter may not deal with the kind of jobs you're targeting. If this is the case, ask if he/she knows a headhunter who does. Start again.
- The headhunter may ask you further questions. This is usually a good sign. Answer as concisely as you can.
- The headhunter may ask you to send in a copy of your CV, again a good sign.

Key points to pick out here are as follows:

- **Headhunters do most of their business on the phone**. You will do better communicating with them in this way than, for example, by writing to them or sending them emails.
- **Connections are important to headhunters.** The name-dropping you do at the start of your conversation will help to focus their attention on what you are saying.
- **Long-windedness is no way to a headhunter's heart.** By coming to the point quickly you will avoid losing the headhunter's interest.

The aim to your approach to the headhunter is twofold:

1 to see whether any of the headhunter's current assignments match up with what you're looking for (an off chance)
2 failing this, to ensure that when your CV arrives it is put in the interesting candidates' file rather than consigned to the batch to be shredded.

Visibility

Headhunters often source candidates from media reports on companies or from other sources that are in the public domain.

> ### Examples
>
> Sean specializes in corporate law and became the target for an approach following an article he wrote for a leading business magazine.
>
> Gemma received three phone calls from headhunters after her name featured prominently in trade press coverage of the launch of her company's latest range of products.

Dealing with headhunters

Once you've got an approach from a headhunter, how should you deal with it? What's the best way of moving the approach forward?

Keep it to yourself

This is the first and most important rule for dealing with approaches. Don't succumb to the temptation to tell everyone. We say this for two good reasons:

- Approaches sometimes fizzle out. This can happen, for example when the company behind the approach changes its mind about recruiting.
- The fact that you've received an approach could send out a message to your principals that you're potentially a short-term stayer, with the result that meaning they're going to think twice before spending any more money on your training and development.

Don't let it go to your head

After an approach there is a tendency to feel flattered.
Someone out there has at last recognized your talents. While
a certain amount of self-satisfaction is only natural, letting an
approach go to your head is fraught with danger. For example:

- if the approach falls through – or you don't get the job for
  any reason – it could deal a crushing blow to your ego
- you could start to view the job with rose-tinted spectacles,
  meaning you fail to pick up on quite glaring mismatches with
  your targeting benchmarks
- feeling flattered tends to go with feeling grateful – not a
  good position to start from when it comes to negotiating the
  best possible deal for yourself.

Don't put up the shutters

Even if you're not looking to make a job move at the moment,
always receive headhunters courteously and hear out what
they've got to say. There are two reasons for this particular
piece of advice:

1 Because of the cost factor alone, jobs filled by headhunting
  tend to be very good jobs – in short, without knowing it, you
  could be turning your back on the opportunity of a lifetime.
  As we all know, opportunity seldom knocks twice.

2 In today's uncertain world, you never know when you're going to need a headhunter. Keeping on the right side of them is therefore in your best interests.

State your position

Aware of the potential for time-wasting, a headhunter will seek to establish at an early stage whether you are in the market for making a move or not. Your response here should be on the lines of: while you're perfectly happy with what you're doing at the moment (true or not), you would always be interested to hear about any opportunities that would move your career forward. Then this cues you up nicely to trot out your targeting benchmarks – including the kind of package it would take to tempt you 'out of your tree' (irrespective of whether a figure has already been mentioned or not.)

 Don't ask for too little!

Employers normally enter into approaches with flexible ideas on the kind of pay and benefits package they would have to put forward to attract the right calibre of candidate. In short, there is usually plenty of latitude for negotiation. Don't, therefore, make the mistake of selling yourself short by naming a figure at the start that's too low.

Remember:

- It is easier to come down than it is to talk your way back up.
- With a top job, you could create the unfortunate impression that you're lacking in personal ambition (a bad point).
- Headhunters are used to talking salaries in truly astronomical figures without the bat of an eyelid. Sentiments like 'being too greedy' or 'going over the top' have little meaning to them.

Move the approach forward

It's usually in your best interests to move the approach forward as quickly as you can and, while the headhunter will probably want to engage you in formal selection procedures such as interviews and psychometric tests, you should endeavour to keep control over the pace at which events move. For example, if the headhunter says 'I'll get back to you', ask for some idea of time scale. If you hear nothing by the date you've been given, then get on the phone and chase them up.

Keeping the approaches coming

The first approach you receive may turn out to be a mismatch but there is a bigger picture here – one where you need the approaches to keep coming at you until eventually the right one turns up. What this means is cultivating headhunters and keeping them sweet. How do you do this? By incorporating some of the lessons we have touched on already, namely:

- **Be courteous.** Never shut the door in a headhunter's face and always hear out what they've got to say.
- **Be available.** Don't make headhunters' lives difficult by being impossible to reach.
- **Be reliable.** Go back to headhunters when you say you will. Don't leave them to have to chase you.
- **Be straight.** If a job's not suitable for you, say so. Don't string headhunters along. Wasting their time won't endear them to you.
- **Be positive.** Tell the headhunter the kind of job you are looking for and what kind of offer would tempt you 'out of the tree'.
- **Be engaging.** Encourage headhunters to keep 'phoning you.
- **Be proactive.** Keep up the contact by 'phoning them from time to time.

Summary

To some, the popular image of headhunting is that it is an extension of the 'old boy network' – the way top jobs in industry and commerce were filled a long time ago. Today you have learned that this is not true. If you have got something to offer to prospective employers, if you have got the right skill set, if you have always done a good job, if you are seen as a safe pair of hands – then someone out there will be interested in you. The social circles you mix in, the school you went to or your family connections will not come into it.

Today you have also taught yourself that, if you want to get headhunted, you need to work on projecting the right image. More to the point, you need to see projecting the right image as something you do every day and not just on special occasions – like going for interviews – or when you feel like it. You have taught yourself to see what you do every day as you go about your business as your lifelong interview. It is the image of you that people carry forward and what will feature prominently the next time a headhunter is deciding whether to give you a call or not.

SUNDAY
MONDAY
TUESDAY
WEDNESDAY
THURSDAY
FRIDAY
SATURDAY

Fact-check (answers at the back)

1. Which of the following is a common reason why firms use headhunters?
   a) It's an inexpensive way of filling positions ☐
   b) They don't want the hassle themselves ☐
   c) It's quicker ☐
   d) They are looking for someone with exceptional qualities to fill a senior position ☐

2. You are quite happy with your current job but you get a phone call one day from an executive search consultant who asks you if you might be interested in a position with one of their clients. How do you respond?
   a) By saying no ☐
   b) By saying it depends on the money ☐
   c) By explaining that you're not looking for another job but, if the move was right for you, you would always be open to discussion ☐
   d) By taking the consultant's phone number and say you will get in touch if your circumstances should change ☐

3. Which of the following is most likely to interest a headhunter?
   a) Your salary expectations are not too high ☐
   b) You can count a number of celebrities among your circle of friends ☐
   c) You have only had one job since you left university ☐
   d) You have no blemishes on your work record or character ☐

4. What is your lifelong interview?
   a) All the experiences you have had at interviews you have attended ☐
   b) The image you project every day ☐
   c) Part of your learning curve ☐
   d) Don't know ☐

5. Which of these is an example of visibility?
   a) Coming to work every day in a different set of clothes ☐
   b) The kind of car you drive ☐
   c) Your blog ☐
   d) A quote from you in a trade journal about a new product your company is launching ☐

6. You receive an approach but a few weeks later the headhunter phones you to say that the position has been put on hold. How do you respond?
   a) By thanking the headhunter for letting you know and making it clear you would still be interested in the position if it came up again ☐
   b) As a), but add on that you would also like to be contacted if the headhunter got to know of any other interesting positions ☐
   c) By asking the headhunter why the position has been put on hold ☐
   d) By telling the headhunter not to ring you again unless the position he/she wants to talk about is more definite ☐

7. A headhunter approaches you about a job that does not interest you. Do you...
a) Pretend to be interested so you do not give the appearance of putting up the shutters? ❏
b) Tell them straight away that you are not interested and explain why? ❏
c) As b), but tell them at the same time what would interest you? ❏
d) Try not to commit yourself? ❏

8. Which of the following is the best way of boosting your chances of being headhunted?
a) Joining the right golf club ❏
b) Working on your lifelong interview ❏
c) Sending your CV to all the firms of executive search consultants you can find on the Internet ❏
d) Starting a blog ❏

9. What should you say when a headhunter asks you how much money you want to be paid?
a) Set out your targeting benchmark ❏
b) Add 20 per cent to your targeting benchmark ❏
c) Say you don't know ❏
d) Ask the headhunter what he/she thinks ❏

10. How do headhunters source candidates?
a) By using their contacts ❏
b) By going through banks of CVs that they hold ❏
c) By advertising on the Internet ❏
d) By getting candidates to register with them ❏

SUNDAY

MONDAY

TUESDAY

WEDNESDAY

THURSDAY

FRIDAY

SATURDAY

Weighing up job offers

Congratulations, you have been offered the job but now you have to decide whether to take it or not. Should you be writing out your resignation or should you be thinking twice?

Today you will learn what to do when the time has come for you to make up your mind. Will the job you have been offered be a good move or are you having second thoughts and, if so, why?

You will also learn that these last-minute worries about changing jobs are not always unfounded. Doubt about what you are doing has crept in from somewhere and, before you hand in your notice, it is sensible to ask yourself why you are hesitating.

Some areas of doubt can be cleared up quickly – often by just by making a phone call. But sometimes your inner voices are telling you more. If you take the job you've been offered, are your new employers trustworthy? How well do you know them? They seemed keen to get you to take the job, even upped the salary, but could this be evidence of their desperation? If so, why are they desperate? Did no one else want the job?

The risk factor

Irrespective of how much research you do into prospective employers, a job move is still largely a step into the unknown. You don't know how you will fit in. You don't know how you will feel about the job in six months' time.

Fears like these serve to deter a lot of people. They turn down perfectly good offers of employment for the simple reason that they develop cold feet. This is clearly no good and a waste of all the time and effort they have put in.

Upsides and downsides

Accepting that there is a risk attached to any change of job, you need to view the risk in its proper context – by which we mean view both the upsides and the downsides together, then stand back and see how they balance up.

- **Upsides:** These are usually the advances in salary you make, the greater challenges and responsibilities the new job has to offer, and so on.
- **Downsides:** These are what happens when the job doesn't work out. You find yourself back on the job market. You could end up making a sideways or even a backwards move to escape from the pain. It could be several years before you get your career back on track.

Downsides are, admittedly, pretty frightening, but what most people neglect to do with their risk assessment is consider another set of upsides and downsides: those associated with turning the job down and staying where they are.

- **Upsides:** You have the security of working for an employer you know.
- **Downsides:** You continue to underachieve, stagnate, be underpaid – whatever it was that drove you out on to the job market in the first place.

Make your job moves for the right reason

There are two golden rules for taking a balanced view of the risks:

1 Don't make job moves for trivial or inconsequential gains (e.g. a small improvement in salary).
2 Don't be driven out on to the job market by minor gripes (e.g. your company car is overdue for a change).

Rogue employers

Not all the creatures you meet in the job jungle will have your best interests at heart. Indeed, the increasing diversity of today's market means that there is a far greater chance of you coming across a few slippery characters on your travels.

We all know of the odd hire-and-fire outfit (employers which are in a constant cycle of taking people on and laying them off), but there are some equally dangerous species about – people who will conceal important facts from you usually to get you to take the job.

How to spot a rogue employer

- Be on your guard the moment you feel you are being 'sold' a job. Good employers always point out the snags as well as the benefits. Rogues confine themselves to painting rosy pictures.

- Beware of employers who make big promises, e.g. on future pay increases – especially when they're not prepared to put their promises into writing.

- Sense danger if the answers to your questions are vague or evasive.

- Watch out for employers who give themselves let-outs – e.g. the offer is made conditional on the retention of a commercial contract.

- Be aware of employers who make you the offer you can't refuse (more on this in a moment).

- Trust your instincts. If you feel there's something fishy about an employer, let that be sufficient reason for you giving them a wide berth. Listen to those inner voices. They rarely let you down.

WARNING!

A lot of jobs today (including management jobs) are short term or temporary, and so you have to be very careful that what you are being offered is indeed a permanent position. Be warned that some unscrupulous employers try to disguise the fact that a job is temporary just to attract suitable applicants.

Weighing up job offers

Though it seems scarcely in need of saying, don't act on any job offer until you've got it in writing. Don't, for example, spread it round the office that you'll be leaving soon. Don't, whatever you do, hand in your notice.

Read the small print

Job offers are frequently quite detailed and/or they come with supporting documentation such as job descriptions, standard terms of employment and information on items such as pension schemes and company cars. Read all of these documents, carefully making notes as you go along.
Pick out:

● any items that you feel need clarification
● anything at variance with information given to you at the interviews
● any items that appear to have been omitted.

What you are safeguarding yourself against here is not so much rogue employers but poor or inexperienced interviewers – people who don't get their facts right or leave out something important (important to you, that is).

Get all the information you need

Again, it scarcely needs saying, but don't accept any job until you've got all the information you need. In most cases this will simply mean a quick phone call to the person who made you the offer, but with really important issues such as the date on which a salary increment becomes payable or the details of a relocation package, it is advisable always to get the additional information put into writing. Any employer who is reluctant to do this should automatically be viewed with suspicion.

Revisit your targeting benchmarks

This, if you like, is your final fail-safe device. Does what you're being offered match up with what you set out to achieve by going out on the job market, or does it fall short in any significant way? Asking yourself this question exposes three potential dangers:

1 You could have allowed your career aims to drift (this tends to happen to people who have been on the job market for a long time). You could have lowered your sights without realizing it.
2 You could be allowing disenchantment with your present job to colour your opinion of what's being offered to you. You could be seeing the new job in a better light than it deserves.
3 You could be succumbing to enticement (read on).

'The perfect job?'

There's no such thing as the perfect job. This is said to warn you against:

- being over-pedantic when it comes to viewing job offers

- turning down good jobs because relatively unimportant aspects of the package are not in line with your expectations.

TIP

Learn to consider your job offers 'in the round'. For example, see where a major improvement in salary (higher than the figure you targeted) far outweighs a slight reduction in holiday entitlement or a more restricted choice of company car.

Enticement

With some employers quite desperate to acquire people with scarce or sought-after skills, the field is wide open for enticement or making an offer in the knowledge that the person on the receiving end will find it hard to refuse. Enticement often goes hand in hand with headhunting.

Enticement is perhaps the commonest reason why people make bad moves. 'I knew it was a mistake,' you hear them saying. 'But, with what was put on the table, how could I say no?'

Enticement can come in many forms: pay, perks and, these days, big upfront lump-sum payments or golden hellos.

All offers are refusable

Needless to say, a job with a fat cat salary and a big flash car won't do you any good at all if it only lasts six months. You should beware of situations therefore where you feel you are being made an offer you can't refuse. OK, it could mean that you've hit the jackpot but it could also mean the employer you're in negotiation with is in dire straits and knows of no other way of getting you to take the job. The message? If the warning bells are ringing out at you, take notice of them.

With job hunting, all that glitters is not gold.

Summary

Today you have learned that the job jungle can be a place full of dangers, especially for the unwary. Some of the creatures you meet may appear to be friendly but, when you get close up to them, you may find out quickly that they are not what they make themselves out to be.

Today you have learned how to spot creatures who could do you harm. But at the same time you have learned not to be put off by employers who are poor interviewers or who give you half the facts because the explanation for these difficulties, in many cases, is pressure of work or lack of experience. You have learned that, where you feel you do not know enough about a job to decide whether you should take it or not, you ask!

Most importantly, today you have learned that, while there is always a risk attached to changing jobs, you should see the risk in terms of its upsides and downsides. Where the upsides outweigh the downsides then it is time to:
- stop agonizing
- get on with the job of writing your notice out.

SUNDAY
MONDAY
TUESDAY
WEDNESDAY
THURSDAY
FRIDAY
SATURDAY

Fact-check (answers at the back)

1. If changing jobs is risky, what do you do to minimize the risk?
   a) Try not to change jobs too often ❑
   b) Nothing – take the risk ❑
   c) Assess the risk properly including the upsides and downsides ❑
   d) Take out more insurance ❑

2. An employer offers you a big salary, far more than the job is worth. What do you read into this?
   a) They value good people ❑
   b) They don't know what they're doing ❑
   c) They are desperate to get someone to take the job ❑
   d) The job won't be there for long ❑

3. A job is offered to you, but in the small print you notice a condition of employment that says you could be asked to work anywhere in the world. The condition wasn't mentioned in any of the interviews, so you phone up and ask for clarification. Even though you are told the condition does not apply to you, you are still concerned. Do you...
   a) Turn the job down? ❑
   b) Ask the employer to put what you have been told into writing? ❑
   c) Accept the job and try to put the concern about being sent anywhere in the world to the back of your mind? ❑
   d) Feel you don't know what to do ❑

4. You find at the final interview stage that a job you've applied for is on a temporary contract for the first 12 months. When you query the arrangement, you are told by the employer that all their jobs start on a temporary contract. Do you...
   a) Withdraw your application? ❑
   b) Go back to the employer and see if they will make the job permanent? ❑
   c) See if you get offered the job? ❑
   d) Complain that you have been misled? ❑

5. You turn a job offer down because you found the owners of the business who interviewed you shifty and evasive. Now they keep coming back to you with bigger and bigger offers of pay. Do you...
   a) Trust your instincts and turn the offers down? ❑
   b) See how far they will go? ❑
   c) Call their bluff and name the offer that you would not be able to refuse? ❑
   d) Ask your partner to decide? ❑

6. You get offered a great job, but then you notice that you will have less holiday entitlement than with your current employer. Do you...
   a) See if you can renegotiate the offer to include more holidays? ❑
   b) Turn the offer down? ❑
   c) Accept the offer as it stands? ❑
   d) As c), but make it plain to your new employer that you have had to sacrifice some of your holidays? ❑

7. You are offered a job but when the negotiations are over you find that the salary falls a long way short of what you originally set out to attain (your targeting benchmark). Do you...

a) Accept the offer because you have not been able to find anything better? ❑

b) Turn it down and carry on looking? ❑

c) As b), but see if the feedback from your job hunting is suggesting that you need to adjust your targeting benchmarks? ❑

d) Turn it down and give your job hunting a rest for a while? ❑

8. You are offered a job but the offer is not very detailed. Do you...

a) Turn the offer down? ❑

b) Go back to the employer and ask them to fill in the missing detail? ❑

c) Take the risk, hand your notice in and hope you can find out all you want to know after you have started? ❑

d) Do nothing and wait for the employer to chase you? ❑

9. You applied for a job because it was advertised with a high salary. You have now been offered the job but on a lower salary than the figure indicated in the advertisement. Do you...

a) Turn the job down in disgust? ❑

b) Go back to your targeting benchmark and see how the offer compares? ❑

c) Ring up the employer and ask why you have not been offered the salary advertised? ❑

d) Feel you could have done better if you had inflated the salary quoted in your CV? ❑

10. What is a golden hello?

a) A pension arrangement for top executives ❑

b) A way of making tax-free payments to high earners ❑

c) An upfront payment made at the start of employment (or in stages) and intended as an enticement device ❑

d) A form of severance payment ❑

Surviving in tough times

Job hunting in difficult times means there will be fewer jobs to go after and more people chasing them. But that isn't all. Business confidence goes down in a recession, so employers faced with replacing leavers or deciding whether a slight upturn in activity calls for taking on an extra member of staff will hesitate. The jobs may be there but they are put on hold as employers wait for signs of a recovery. Here are ten tips for job hunting in a recession which take account of these changed conditions and which you will be able to use to your advantage.

1 Look for growth sectors

Not all businesses are affected by downturns and there will always be some who manage to buck the trends. Make an effort to identify businesses which are buoyant as part of your sourcing. If they are not advertising, try cold-calling them or sending in an unsolicited CV. A lot of these businesses will be SMEs (small to medium-sized enterprises) which may be good at whatever it is they do but less adept when it comes to recruiting. Here is where you might get your chance.

2 Focus on the invisible market

In recessionary times many employers hold back when it comes to recruiting but an interesting unsolicited CV arriving in the post or by email is often all it takes to make them change their minds. This is the power of proactive sourcing, which is a particularly effective tool when otherwise the job scene looks bleak. Revisit the chapters in the book that deal with the invisible market and how to access it.

3 Tap into your networks

Now is the time to pull a few strings. When job market conditions are difficult, professional networking is one of the best ways of accessing opportunities. So sound out your circle of contacts and see what they can come up with. As you have read in this book, networking is a particularly good way of accessing the invisible market, and in recessionary times you will find a lot more happening in the invisible market than in its visible counterpart.

4 Widen your targets

Targeting a narrow range of jobs when you are out of work or when your job is under threat is obviously not sensible. However, even in these circumstances, your job hunting still needs a sense of direction. Overcome this difficulty by having more than one target – for example, the job you would really like to get and the job you would be prepared to accept in the short term. In theory, you can have as many targets as you like, but in practice you might find too many targets difficult to manage.

5 Revisit your CV

When there are dozens if not hundreds of applicants chasing every job that is advertised, employers will be inundated with CVs. You have learned from this book the importance of making your CV a quick and easy read but there is always room for improvement. Pay particular attention if you find you are not getting interviews. It could be the other candidates are better than you, but equally it could be your CV has failed the instant accessibility test. This is something you can easily put right.

6 Don't hang about

We have warned you in this book about the dangers of procrastinating when you are applying for jobs that have been advertised. When there are a lot of people looking for jobs, you can take it as read that the employer concerned will be swamped with applications. What can happen is that the ones that come in later don't get read. The message here is simple. Get your application off straight away, even if it means burning the midnight oil.

7 Learn to take the knocks

Even in better times job hunters have to learn to take the knocks, but when market conditions are difficult the knocks are more frequent. Here it helps to remind yourself that applying for jobs in the thick of a recession is never going to be easy and, unless you are very fortunate, the effort you have to put in (and keep putting in) must be sustained over long periods of time. What you need to do, therefore, is to adjust your thinking and learn to treat the negative experiences as the norm – that is, as something you put behind you and move on from, rather than as something that eats away at you and undermines your determination to carry on.

8 Keep in control

In this book there are a number of examples of how you can steer your job hunting to successful conclusions by keeping in control. Keeping in control and forcing the pace of events is especially important where employers are not in a hurry to fill positions, as is often the case in a recession. So, if anyone is going to ring up to fix the next interview, make sure it's you. 'Don't ring us, we'll ring you' is what employers used to say. Now it's time to turn the tables.

9 Be careful

On Saturday we looked at the risks which go with changing jobs. In a recession there is a greater risk of moving to a job which doesn't last long. The business fails or it has to make cuts and you find yourself facing redundancy. The bottom line here is that, if you are in a good job which is relatively secure, you need to think carefully before making a step into the unknown.

10 Keep your options open

We live in a world which is uncertain and, for this reason, it is important to keep your options open and have irons in the fire all the time. Hopefully, your job hunting will have a happy ending and you will find the job you are looking for, but the advice to stay in touch with the job market still holds good. When one downturn is over there is usually another not far behind, so, if you follow our advice, the next time you need to engage with the job market you won't be in the position of having to make a cold start.

Conclusion
Job hunting as a part of a career strategy

Job hunting for many people is something they turn to in moments of desperation. They do it, for example, when their jobs are put at risk or when the pressure starts to get too much for them. They do it when the pay rise they banked on doesn't materialize or when they get passed by for promotion. Desperation puts pressure on people to go for quick solutions. They end up taking the first decent offer that comes along. This means that:

- they're not on the job market for very long
- they only ever see a fragment of the complete range of opportunities available to them
- they build up little or no experience.

Bearing in mind that these short spells of frantic job hunting are usually interspersed by long periods of inactivity, the result is a view of the outside world that is rather like a series of snapshots – one where you only see:

- what's in the frame, *and*
- what's happening at one particular point in time.

Keep the job opportunities coming

The two main messages in this book are:

1 There's a much bigger market out there for your talents than you think.
2 Source the bigger market properly and you could profit from it handsomely.

There is one final piece to the infrastructure we need to put into place, however, and it is this. You need to have an on-going view of what the market has to offer, not one that starts and stops depending on how life happens to be treating you at the time. In other words, this is where you ditch the series of snapshots and go into moving pictures.

How do you do this? The answer is by employing some of the lessons we have touched on during the course of this week:

● **Don't be driven out on the job market by desperation.**
● **Keep in contact with the visible market** by scanning the ads regularly. As a matter of course, apply for any good jobs that catch your eye.

- **Keep up the proactive sourcing.** Keep up your presence on the invisible market by staying on the books of selected recruitment consultants. Mailshot selected employers occasionally.
- **Keep your networks open.** Let it be known to your contacts that you are always interested in hearing about opportunities.
- **Keep working on your lifelong interview.** Make yourself a more attractive target to headhunters by continuing to project a person-perfect and work-perfect image.
- **Encourage headhunters to keep calling you.** Don't put them off by being negative with them.

Because of the uncertainties of the world in which we live, good career management is about keeping options open and having irons in the fire all of the time. Keep on-line with the job market. Turn job hunting into an everyday part of your life.

What have you have learned this week?

- Job hunting benefits from having your ideas thought out clearly first.
- Source the whole market and not just part of it.
- Don't miss out on the invisible market and what it's got to offer.
- Do everything you can to make yourself a target for headhunters.
- Be selective with the jobs you go for.
- Learn to leave some jobs alone.
- Make job hunting part of every day.

A final word

When everything seems to be going against you, shooting off a few job applications immediately makes you feel better. You are doing something positive. Avenues are opening up. The world is suddenly a bigger and more exciting place..

Answers

Sunday: 1c; 2a; 3d; 4b; 5c; 6c; 7d; 8c; 9b; 10d.

Monday: 1c; 2d; 3b; 4a; 5d; 6a; 7d; 8c; 9c; 10b.

Tuesday: 1d; 2c; 3b; 4a; 5b; 6a; 7c; 8a; 9b; 10c.

Wednesday: 1a; 2b; 3d; 4a; 5b; 6c; 7c (or a); 8a; 9d; 10d.

Thursday: 1b; 2a; 3d; 4c; 5c; 6c; 7a (or d); 8b; 9c; 10b.

Friday: 1d; 2c; 3d; 4b; 5d; 6b; 7c; 8b; 9b; 10a.

Saturday: 1c; 2c and d; 3b; 4a; 5a; 6c; 7c; 8b; 9b; 10c.